P9-EER-782

UNFINISHED SYMPHONY

and other Stories of Men and Music

UNFINISHED SYMPHONY

and other
Stories of Men and Music

FREDA BERKOWITZ

drawings by Joseph Schindelman

Atheneum New York
1963

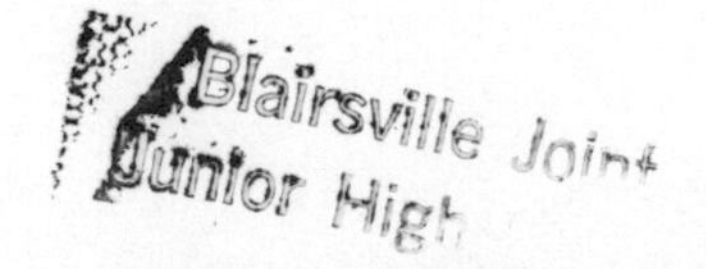

We gratefully acknowledge permission to reproduce the following musical selections:

POMP AND CIRCUMSTANCE NO. 1, Elgar, arranged for piano by Eugene Valber
Copyright 1943 by Boosey & Company Ltd.
Reprinted by permission of Boosey & Hawkes Inc.

THE CAT AND THE MOUSE (8 measures starting 11 from the end), Copland
Copyright 1921 by Durand et Cie. Renewed 1949
Copyright assigned 1950 to Boosey & Hawkes Inc. for USA
Reprinted by permission of Boosey & Hawkes Inc.

EL SALÓN MÉXICO (5 measures starting 4 bars after 8), Copland
Copyright 1939 by Hawkes & Son (London) Ltd.
Reprinted by permission of Boosey & Hawkes Inc.

BILLY THE KID (the 1st 7 solo piccolo measures), Copland
Copyright 1941 by Hawkes & Son (London) Ltd.
Reprinted by permission of Boosey & Hawkes Inc.

THE SECOND HURRICANE (1st 13 measures of Soprano Solo of Pupil's Chorus), Copland
Copyright 1938 by C. C. Birchard & Co.
Copyright assigned to Boosey & Hawkes Inc. 1957
Reprinted by permission of Boosey & Hawkes Inc.

VARIATION 24 OF RAPSODIE ON A THEME OF PAGANINI, Rachmaninoff
Copyright 1934 by Charles Foley Inc., New York
Used by permission

Music examples prepared by MAXWELL WEANER

Library of Congress catalog card number 63–10372
Published simultaneously in Canada by McClelland & Stewart Ltd.
MANUFACTURED IN THE UNITED STATES OF AMERICA
PRINTED BY *Connecticut Printers Inc., Hartford*
BOUND BY *H. Wolff, New York*
FIRST EDITION

To my grandchildren

GREGORY *and* PETER

Introduction

Sometimes in music there are nicknames for musical compositions just as people have nicknames. A boy whose name is Gregory might be called "Butch," and he can become so accustomed to that nickname that he may even answer to it faster than he does to his real name. A piece of music like the Beethoven piano sonata called Sonata in C♯ Minor, Op. 27, No. 2 has been nicknamed *Moonlight Sonata*. That nickname is much better known than the real name.

In the first part of this book, the stories will tell you how some musical compositions have received their nicknames. In the second part of the book you will find sketches of the lives of the composers whose stories you read about.

Contents

PART I—STORIES OF MUSIC

Contents

PART II—STORIES OF MEN

Stories OF MUSIC

ACADEMIC FESTIVAL OVERTURE

Overture for Orchestra in C Minor, Op. 80

JOHANNES BRAHMS

When people go to a university they often have to write a long paper on a special subject in order to get a Master's or Doctor's Degree. This paper is called a *thesis*.

The great German composer, Johannes Brahms, was given an honorary degree of Doctor of Philosophy from the University of Breslau in the spring of 1879. Instead of writing his *thesis* in words, he wrote it in music. It was not at all a serious piece, as one might expect; instead it was a jolly mixture of student songs. When you listen to this piece, it is easy to imagine students standing around and singing and perhaps even drinking steins of beer.

Brahms must have had a twinkle in his eye and a smile on his face when he jokingly called his *thesis* *Academic Festival Overture*.

AEOLIAN HARP

Étude for Piano in A♭ Major, Op. 25 No. 1

FREDERIC CHOPIN

The name for the real aeolian harp comes from Aeolus, the Greek god of the winds. The instrument has strings stretched over a long narrow sound box and, when the wind hits the strings, they vibrate and make musical sounds. These sounds are something like the sounds of the harp.

If you have ever listened to a harp, you will remember that much of the music gives the impression of broken flowing chords running up and down the instrument.

In this étude for the piano, Chopin tried to imitate the sound of the harp. When Robert Schumann, another great composer, heard Chopin play the piece, he said that it reminded him of an aeolian harp. Ever since that time the nickname *Aeolian Harp* has been used for this étude.

There is still another nickname that is given to this piece. It is called *Shepherd Boy Étude*.

The story is that Chopin told one of his pupils that when he wrote this piece he had imagined a little shepherd taking refuge in a grotto during a storm. In order to pass the time away, the little boy played a flowing melody on his flute.

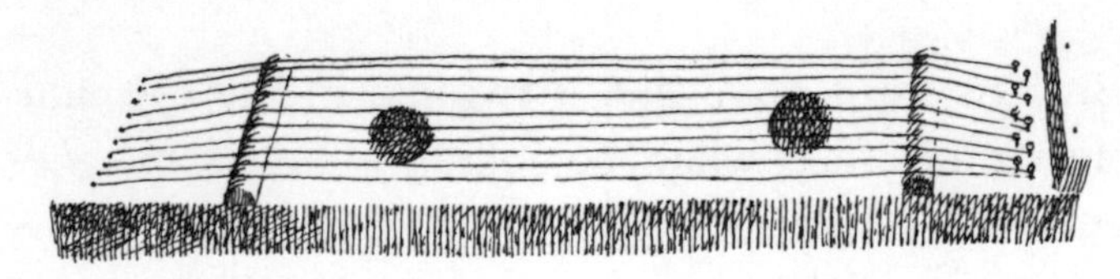

AMERICAN QUARTET

Quartet for Strings in F Major, Op. 96

ANTON DVOŘÁK

Anton Dvořák, the Bohemian composer, visited the United States from 1892 to 1895.

While in this country, Dvořák listened to a great deal of American folk music. He particularly loved the music of the Negroes and the Indians.

Among Dvořák's pupils at the National Conservatory in New York was a man called H. T. Burleigh. He was a prominent Negro baritone, and he spent long hours with Dvořák, singing and playing many Negro spirituals and slave songs for him.

When Dvořák wrote this quartet, he remembered many of the folk melodies he had heard and when you listen to the music you can hear that he was influenced by the tunes and their rhythms. Because of this, the quartet has always been known by its nickname *American Quartet*.

APPASSIONATA

Sonata for Piano in F Minor, Op. 57

LUDWIG VAN BEETHOVEN

Beethoven was a very emotional man. He could be happy one minute and sad the next. He also had violent fits of temper.

In the first movement of this sonata, Beethoven seems

to be in a fury from start to finish. The second movement is calm and beautiful; but suddenly, without any pause, the third movement begins with chords that sound like claps of thunder. The music continues in this stormy fashion until the end.

Some people raise their voices and scold when they get in a temper, but Beethoven raised his voice in his music. When you listen to the music, you can almost see Beethoven pacing up and down his room completely shaken with his emotions. He could not rest until he had written this powerful music.

Although Beethoven himself did not nickname this sonata *Appassionata,* it was a most appropriate one. It was Cranz, the music publisher, in Hamburg, Germany, who gave it this nickname.

ARCHDUKE TRIO

Trio for Piano, Violin and 'Cello in B♭ Major, Op. 97

LUDWIG VAN BEETHOVEN

The Archduke Rudolph of Austria studied the piano with Beethoven. He also was a friend of Beethoven. Because of this, Beethoven decided to write a special piece for the Archduke. In only three weeks he wrote this trio for piano, violin, and 'cello.

Rudolph was so anxious to play the piece that he did not wait for the music to be copied. It is difficult to read music right from the manuscript, but the Archduke and his friends worked until they were able to play it.

This trio is still played quite often. It has always been known by its nickname *Archduke Trio.*

THE BATTLE

Symphony Op. 91

LUDWIG VAN BEETHOVEN

When the Duke of Wellington won a victory over Napoleon's forces at Vittoria, Spain, Beethoven wrote this symphony to celebrate the occasion.

He first wrote it for a new instrument, the Panharmonicon. This instrument was invented by Beethoven's friend, Maelzel, who was also the inventor of the metronome. This metronome is still used a great deal as a mechanical time-beater, but the Panharmonicon never became either popular or practical.

It was a tremendous instrument which was really a mechanical brass band, all contained in a single case. It was impossible to move such a gigantic instrument from concert hall to concert hall. When Beethoven was finally convinced that this was so, he took the music and arranged it for orchestra. He not only used a full orchestra, but also doubled the basses and drums.

The audience was so excited after they heard this symphony for the first time, that they cheered and cheered. Beethoven became a popular hero.

This symphony made more of an impression on many in the audience than all of the seven symphonies that Beethoven had composed up until this time.

Sometimes this piece is nicknamed *The Battle*. Other times it is called *The Battle of Vittoria*. It even has a third nickname, *Wellington's Victory*.

Even though it was a sensation when it was first performed, nowadays it is hardly ever played.

THE BEAR

Symphony No. 82 in C Major

JOSEPH HAYDN

The last movement of this symphony is what gives us a clue to its nickname.

The music begins with the big string basses grumbling on a low C. This keeps up for several measures while the rest of the orchestra plays a rhythmic dance. In the music of the dance, the oboes and the bassoons imitate the sounds of bagpipes.

As the music plays, it is easy to imagine a big brown bear grunting and dancing. Perhaps the audience in Paris who heard this symphony for the first time felt the same way. It was said that it was this audience who nicknamed the symphony *L'Ours* or *The Bear*.

Here are a few bars of the music that show the heavy, plodding bear:

THE BIRD

String Quartet No. 3 in C Major, Op. 33
(*Russian Quartets*)

JOSEPH HAYDN

Many times composers try to imitate the sounds of birds in their music. In this quartet Haydn got the effect of birds by writing short notes which are played very quickly. These notes are called *grace notes.*

In the first theme of the first movement of this quartet there are many of these little grace notes which are played by all four instruments. Again in the trio, or middle part, of another movement, there is a charming duet between the first and second violins. This really gives the effect of the twittering sounds of birds.

It was the four men who played this quartet for the first time in the year 1781 who nicknamed it *The Bird.*

Here is a little of the music:

BLACK KEY ÉTUDE

Étude for Piano in G♭ Major, Op. 10 No. 5

FREDERIC CHOPIN

When Chopin wrote this étude for piano, he decided to give most of the work to the black keys, the sharps and flats. In fact, there is only one time in the right hand that a white key is played.

The beginning of this étude is:

BRANDENBURG CONCERTOS

Six Concertos for Orchestra

JOHANN SEBASTIAN BACH

The Margrave of Brandenburg was a prince who loved music. He particularly loved concertos. In modern times we would call him a "concerto fan." He met Johann Sebastian Bach in 1719 and he was enchanted with both Bach's playing and his compositions. Since the Margrave had his own orchestra, he asked Bach to write some music for him.

Two years later Bach had composed six concertos for the Margrave. Each of the concertos was for stringed instruments, but each of them had different instruments playing the solo parts.

The first concerto had 2 horns, 3 oboes, and a bassoon as solo instruments. The second had a flute, an oboe, a trumpet, and a violin. The third was all for strings. The fourth used 1 violin and 2 flutes for solo instruments. The fifth had piano, one flute, and one violin; and the sixth used 2 violas, 2 gambas, and a 'cello.

A gamba was an instrument very much like the 'cello; it was in use before the 'cello was invented.

Because of the following dedication, these concertos have always been known as *The Brandenburg Concertos.*

"As I had the honour of playing before Your Royal Highness a couple of years ago, and as I observed that you took some pleasure in the small talent that Heaven has given me for music, and in taking leave of your Royal Highness you honoured me with a command to bring to you some pieces of my composition, I now, according to Your gracious orders, take the liberty of presenting my very humble respect to your Royal Highness, with the present concertos, which I have written for several instruments, humbly praying you not to judge their imperfection by the severity of the fine and delicate taste that everyone knows you to have for music, but rather to consider benignly the profound respect and the very humble obedience to which they are meant to testify. For the rest, Monseigneur, I very humbly beg your Royal Highness to have the goodness to continue your good grace towards me, and to be convinced that I have nothing so much at heart as the wish to be employed in matters more worthy of you and your service, for with zeal unequalled, Monseigneur,

I am
Your Royal Highness's most humble
and most obedient servant
Jean Sebastian Bach
Cöthen 24 Mar. (March? May?) 1721"

It is not known how the Margrave rewarded Bach for his present, but it is known that when the Margrave died they were said to be worth twenty-four groschen. In those days eight groschen were worth $1.50, which makes the value $4.50 for six of the finest pieces in all of music.

BUTTERFLY

Étude for Piano in G♭ Major, Op. 10 No. 5

FREDERIC CHOPIN

Chopin wrote twenty-seven études or *studies* for the piano. This one is light and beautiful. You can well imagine a butterfly spreading its wings and flying about when you listen to it played.

As is true with most of the nicknames for Chopin pieces, it is difficult to know who started the name. We think that it probably was one of his publishers. As far as this étude is concerned, it could not have a more appropriate nickname.

CAT'S FUGUE

Fugue for Harpsichord in D Minor

DOMENICO SCARLATTI

The Italian composer Domenico Scarlatti, had a cat who loved to walk over the keyboard of his harpsichord. One day while Scarlatti was composing, his cat jumped up on the keys and with his paw struck certain notes one by one. This inspired the composer to write a fugue.

A *fugue* is a piece of music which has several parts or *voices*. It is built on a melody called a *subject*. First the subject is announced by itself and then it is imitated in the other voices, one after the other. Whenever a new voice plays the subject, the other voices go on playing something else. In this way all the voices play together.

Because this fugue is built on the subject that the pussycat "composed," it was given the name it carries.

THE CAT AND THE MOUSE

Scherzo Humoristique, Piece for Piano

AARON COPLAND

The American composer, Aaron Copland, wrote this humorous piece more than forty years ago when he was living in Brooklyn, New York. It is really a scherzo, and a *scherzo* is a musical joke. Mr. Copland cannot remember whether he thought of calling it *The Cat and the Mouse* before or after composing the music. As a matter of fact, he thinks that perhaps "they were born together." Whatever the circumstances were, Mr. Copland could not have found a more appropriate name.

The music begins rather quietly as the cat is walking into the living room. Suddenly he spies a little mouse under the rocking chair and he dashes across the room. As they chase each other around and around, the music becomes very lively. Each time the cat thinks he has the mouse in his clutches, the mouse escapes just in time. The cat, about to forget the whole thing, suddenly sits up and with a sly expression, which seems to say "I must think of a way to outsmart that tiny good-for-nothing," begins his chase once again. As the cat creeps up when the mouse least expects it, the music is sinister and mysterious. The chase becomes more exciting, and the music becomes faster and faster. Alas, for our little friend, the mouse, the cat finally is the winner.

The proud cat limps away, exhausted but triumphant.

Here are a few measures of the sad music at the end of *The Cat and the Mouse*.

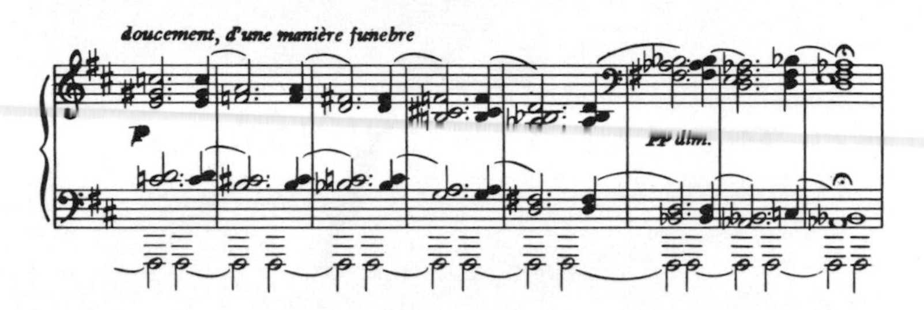

CAT'S WALTZ

Waltz for Piano in F Major, Op. 34 No. 3

FREDERIC CHOPIN

One day while Chopin was in the middle of composing this Waltz No. 3 in F Major, his cat jumped up on the piano and ran up and down the keys. Chopin was so amused by the sound that he tried to get the same effect in the music he was writing.

In the fourth section of this waltz there are many small notes called appoggiaturas. *Appoggiaturas* are small notes that are played very quickly. As a matter of fact, they are played so quickly that they sound as if they are struck at the same time as the following note. The sound is similar to the meowings of a cat.

THE CLOCK

Symphony No. 101 In D Major

JOSEPH HAYDN

In the slow movement of this symphony, there is a section played by bassoons and strings. Instead of the strings having a bow drawn across them, they are plucked with the finger. This is called *pizzicato*. The low sounds of the bassoons, together with this regular plucked sound of the strings give the impression of the ticking of a large clock. In one part the tick tock sound becomes softer, and for this effect Haydn uses the flutes. Perhaps, in this section, he was trying to imitate the ticking of a small clock.

Another reason this symphony is nicknamed *The Clock* is that the minuet movement was originally composed by Haydn for a musical clock.

COFFEE CANTATA

Cantata No. 211 Schweigt stille plaudert nicht (Be silent, don't chatter)

JOHANN SEBASTIAN BACH

In the eighteenth century there were many princes who forbade the drinking of coffee in their dominions.

Some people thought that this was very amusing and even wrote stories about it. Picander, who was a writer in the time of Bach, wrote such a story.

In the story, a father called Mr. Schlendrian wanted

to break his daughter, Lieschen, of the coffee habit. She loved coffee very much, and she pleaded with him, saying, "If I do not drink my little cup of coffee three times a day, I shall be like a dried up piece of roast goat's flesh." Her father still tried to convince her that coffee was bad for her. Finally Lieschen said, "Well, dear father, I will obey you if you find a nice rich husband for me."

Mr. Schlendrian was delighted with his daughter's decision. As he was preparing to go off on a search for a husband, Lieschen again changed her mind. This time she said, "I will not marry any suitor unless the marriage agreement will permit me to have coffee whenever I want it."

Bach was particularly amused by this story because the pet name of his daughter Elizabeth was "Lieschen."

He based his Cantata *Schweigt stille plaudert nicht* (*Be silent, don't chatter*) on Picander's story. Although we never discover whether or not Lieschen's wish came true, we do get a good laugh when we listen to the words and music of this composition.

Because of the story, the cantata was given the nickname by which it is always known, the *Coffee Cantata*.

CORONATION

Concerto for Piano and Orchestra in D Major, K. 537

Wolfgang Amadeus Mozart

The coronation of a king has always been an important and exciting occasion. In October, 1790, Leopold II of Tuscany was to be crowned emperor at

Frankfurt, Germany. Mozart knew that the city would swarm with people from all over Germany, come to see the coronation. He felt that this would be a wonderful time to give concerts. He was right. The audiences were large and enthusiastic. At one of these concerts he played a concerto that he had actually composed three years before.

In order to make the piece more brilliant and really give it a royal ring, Mozart added trumpets and tympani to the score.

Because the first important performance of the concerto was for such a festive occasion, Johann André, Mozart's publisher, nicknamed it *Coronation Concerto.*

CRÈME DE MENTHE

Twenty-fourth Variation of "Rhapsody on a Theme of Paganini"

SERGEI RACHMANINOFF

This is the story of a piece of music which is nicknamed after a drink called *Crème de Menthe.*

Sergei Rachmaninoff was a Russian pianist and composer. One evening when he was at a dinner party, he met his friend Benno Moisewitsch, who was also a pianist. During their conversation Rachmaninoff told his friend about a new piece he had written that he was going to perform in a few weeks. There was one variation, the last one, that was terribly difficult. To play certain chords, the hands had to jump quite suddenly from one part of the piano to another. To make it even more difficult, the hands jumped in opposite directions. Rachmaninoff, himself, could never be sure if the jumps would come out correctly. As they talked, a butler came around with a tray of liqueurs. Rachmaninoff, who never drank liqueurs, refused. Moisewitsch looked at him and said, "Sergei, don't you know that the best thing in the world for jumps is a drink of crème de menthe?" Rachmaninoff drank some, went to the piano, and to his amazement all the jumps were perfect.

Not only did Rachmaninoff always take a little crème de menthe before playing this piece, but he nicknamed the twenty-fourth variation *Crème de Menthe.*

DEVIL'S TRILL SONATA

Sonata for Violin and Piano in G Major

GIUSEPPE TARTINI

One night in the year 1713 the Italian violinist and composer Giuseppe Tartini had a strange dream. He dreamt that he had made an agreement with the devil, who promised to be at his service on all occasions. Before the dream was over, Tartini gave the devil a violin, just to see if the devil was smart enough to play something. To Tartini's surprise, the devil played so beautifully and with such skill that the music was superior to all the music the composer had ever heard. Just then he awoke. He jumped off his bed at once and seized his violin, trying to play what he had heard. However, not only had the devil disappeared but also the exact music that he had played.

Nevertheless, when Tartini got over his feverish excitement, he sat down and composed this difficult and beautiful piece for the violin. He nicknamed it *Devil's Trill Sonata.*

DRUM ROLL

Symphony No. 103 in E♭ Major

Joseph Haydn

There is an anecdote about Haydn and his love of the drums. When he was a very small boy, he was asked to beat the drums in a procession. He was so little that the drum had to be lowered to his height and carried in front of him by a hunchback. This incident began a life long interest in the drums. Many, many years later, when Haydn visited London, he occasionally played the drums at the famous Salamon Concerts.

These concerts were arranged by a violinist and producer of musical programs, Johann Peter Salamon. He was a clever man. He knew that bringing Haydn back to England, where he had been a success before, would attract many people to his concerts. Haydn was invited and was also asked to compose new music especially for the Salamon Concerts. As Salamon had anticipated large audiences came to the concerts.

This symphony is one of twelve that Haydn composed for the Salamon Concerts. The beginning of the symphony is different from anything Haydn had written before. There is a long solo drum roll at the start of the first movement, which undoubtedly is the reason for its well-known nickname.

THE EMPEROR

Concerto for Piano No. 5 in E♭ Major, Op. 73

Ludwig van Beethoven

During the year 1809, when this concerto was written, Napoleon's armies invaded Vienna. Beethoven was not only angered by this attack on his beloved city, but he suffered great physical anguish as well. He was not as yet completely deaf, and his ears were sensitive. He could not stand the noise of the bombarding guns. For days he had to hide in the cellar and cover his ears.

The music of the Fifth Piano Concerto is grand and powerful from the very first measures. Because it is the most powerful of all of Beethoven's piano concertos, it is easy to understand why the nickname *Emperor* was given to it.

However, Beethoven hated Napoleon for the dreadful things that he was doing to Vienna and never would have permitted the concerto to be called the *Emperor Concerto*.

There is a feeling that the music publisher J. B. Cramer was responsible for the nickname.

THE EMPEROR

Quartet for Strings in C Major, Op. 76 No. 3

JOSEPH HAYDN

Haydn wrote a song which became the Austrian National Anthem. It was called *Gott Erhalte Franz den Kaiser*. (*"God Keep Franz, the Emperor."*)

God Keep Franz, the Emperor was a great favorite of Haydn. And so, when he was writing this string quartet, he decided to use the melody of the hymn for the theme of the slow movement. On this theme he wrote beautiful variations which make up the movement. The whole quartet takes its name from the use of this theme in the one part of the work.

There is a famous story about this theme and an incident that happened at the end of his life when he was very ill. He called his servants to come and carry him to the piano. When they seated him at the instrument, he solemnly played the *Emperor's Hymn* three times in succession. It was the last time he ever played. Five days later, May 31, 1809, he died.

ENIGMA VARIATIONS

Variations on an Original Theme, Op. 36

SIR EDWARD ELGAR

One day Sir Edward Elgar, an English composer, was sitting at his piano, improvizing. He suddenly got the idea for a special kind of piece, a theme and fourteen variations written in the form of a puzzle.

There are two mysteries involved in this composition. The first of these is still unsolved. The theme of this piece is based, in part, on a musical composition that Sir Edward said everyone knew. No one has so far been able to guess what this is. The composer died in 1934 without having told what this piece was. Musicians and music lovers still listen and try to guess, however, even though no one will ever know for sure what Elgar had in mind.

The second mystery has been solved. At the top of each of the fourteen variations is an initial or a make-believe name for one of Elgar's friends. Because the music so cleverly describes something special about each friend, each one's real name has been discovered.

EROICA

Symphony No. 3 in E♭ Major, Op. 55

LUDWIG VAN BEETHOVEN

In the very early 1800's, Beethoven was much impressed by the achievements of Napoleon. He thought that Napoleon was a true friend of all the people and a great hero. In honor of Napoleon Beethoven composed his Third Symphony which became known as the *Eroica*.

The way in which Beethoven used the brass instruments in the first movement of the symphony gives the feeling of the great power of Napoleon.

When Beethoven had finished the symphony and it was ready to be sent to Paris to be published, however, the news arrived that Napoleon had proclaimed himself Emperor. Beethoven was beside himself with disappointment. He flew into a rage and cried out, "Is then he, too, nothing more than an ordinary human being? Now he, too, will trample on all the rights of man and indulge only his ambition. . . ." In a fury, he tore out the dedication to Napoleon and substituted "To the Memory of a Great Man."

In Vienna, in the musical archives (where much important musical information is kept) the original page can be seen. There is a ragged hole where Napoleon's name once stood.

FAREWELL SYMPHONY

Symphony No. 45 in F♯ Minor (sometimes called Candle Symphony)

JOSEPH HAYDN

There are two quite different stories as to why this symphony has been nicknamed *Farewell Symphony*.

The first is the one that has been accepted for many years.

At the time that Haydn wrote the *Farewell Sym-*

phony, he was employed by Prince Nicholas for his Esterháza Estate. This was a summer residence; but the musicians spent the greater part of the year there, providing entertainment whenever the Prince or guests were present.

The castle at Esterháza was large and beautiful. Haydn and the men in his orchestra had everything they wanted. There was just one thing that they were not happy about. They could not have their families with them because the living quarters provided for the musicians were not large enough.

Haydn finally decided on a scheme that would tell the Prince, through music, how anxious the men were to go home to their families. The last movement of the symphony he composed for the occasion starts in a lively fashion, but suddenly the music becomes very slow. The Prince could not understand the reason for this, but what followed puzzled him even more. One by one, the men stopped playing, blew out their candles, and calmly walked off the stage. Only two men remained. They were Haydn and the Prince's favorite violinist, Tomasini. Finally, the Prince seemed to understand what was happening and said, "If they go, we may as well go, too." The next day the whole court left, and everyone was happy.

In the other story Haydn was supposed to have heard that the Prince was going to dismiss all the musicians. This made Haydn sad. He wrote the *Farewell Symphony* to try to make the Prince change his mind and not say, "farewell." When the Prince heard this beautiful music, he was so moved that he decided to let the musicians remain in Esterháza after all.

FATE SYMPHONY

Symphony No. 5 in C Minor, Op. 67

Ludwig van Beethoven

This symphony is played so often that few people have not heard at least part of it on a record, the radio, television, or at a concert. The first four notes are ggge♭. The dramatic way in which Beethoven uses these notes gives the impression of a knock at the door.

One day, during a conversation with his friend and biographer, Anton Schindler, Beethoven is supposed to have said, concerning this symphony, "Thus Fate knocks at the door."

During the second World War, 1939–1945, this symphony was called by still another nickname, *The Victory Symphony*. There are several reasons for this. First, the V (Symphony No. V) is a symbol for victory. The second reason is that V in the Morse Code is . . . — . The similarity in rhythm between the code and the first four notes of the symphony is easy to hear. During the war, people whistled these first four notes as a message of hope and encouragement.

FROM THE NEW WORLD

Symphony in E Minor, Op. 95

ANTON DVOŘÁK

During Anton Dvořák's three year stay in the United States, he composed several important pieces of music. One of the most popular of these compositions is the symphony nicknamed *From the New World.*

There is no doubt that Dvořák was influenced by his love of Negro and Indian folk music, to which he listened during his stay in America, but he did not weave in the actual melodies.

Some people feel that the real reason for Dvořák's nicknaming this Symphony *From the New World* is that this beautiful music expressed his loneliness for his own country, Bohemia.

Here is a little bit about the music itself.

The symphony opens with a slow phrase for the string and wood-wind instruments. The second theme of the first movement was undoubtedly inspired by the

Negro spiritual *Swing Low, Sweet Chariot*. The second movement of the symphony is the famous *Largo*. The main melody of this movement is played by the English horn and is said to be one of the most beautiful in all of music. The third movement is a scherzo, and the fourth begins with a march-like melody.

Even if you have never heard the complete symphony, you may know the famous *Largo* movement. Words have been written for it, and it is sung in the schools under the title *Goin' Home*.

FÜR ELISE

Bagatelle for Piano in A Minor

Ludwig van Beethoven

In the year 1810, Beethoven was very much in love with a young lady named Therese Malfatti. He hoped to marry her. And it was for her that he wrote this piece. Unfortunately, her family objected to the match and the marriage did not take place. The piece was somehow cast aside.

Some years later Beethoven's first biographer, Ludwig Nohl, was looking through books and papers in the estate of a friend of Therese Malfatti. Quite by accident he found the same little piece. He misread the dedication which said "für Therese am 27 April zur Erinnerung an L. V. Bthon" ("For Therese the 27 April as a remembrance from L. V. Beethoven"). He understood it to say *Für Elise* ("For Elise"). Poor Therese! Beethoven did not marry her, and the millions who know this charming little work call it by another's name.

This is the beginning of *Für Elise*.

THE GHOST TRIO

Trio in D Major, Op. 70

LUDWIG VAN BEETHOVEN

When Beethoven read the play *Macbeth* by William Shakespeare, he was very much impressed by it and started to write an opera based on it.

In the play there is a scene called "The Witch's Scene." Beethoven must have been thinking of this when he wrote *The Ghost Trio*.

We feel fairly certain that this was so, because in his original notebook he wrote opera music for the scene and on the same page he wrote the music for the trio. The trio was not part of the opera music, but both were influenced by Shakespeare's play.

In the second movement of the trio there is a weird, almost frightening melody, which comes back several times. It actually sounds like a ghostly voice. Beethoven had never written such eerie music before. It might have been nicknamed *The Ghost Trio,* even if there was not such a good reason for doing so.

GOLDBERG VARIATIONS

Air and Thirty Variations for Harpsichord

JOHANN SEBASTIAN BACH

In the time of Bach, composers were asked to write music for many different occasions. This was one way they had of making money. Wealthy men had the music written sometimes for reasons that seem very funny to us today.

The Russian Ambassador to the Court of Dresden, Count Hermann Karl von Kayserling, had great difficulty sleeping. Because he loved music, he hired famous performers to play for him at night. These men always had a room next to his and had to get up and play when he called to them.

At one particular time, J. T. Theodore Goldberg, who was a marvellous harpsichord player, was hired to fill this position. This young man was Johann Sebastian Bach's best pupil. Count Kayserling asked Bach to write a piece that Goldberg could play for him during his sleepless nights.

Bach set to work with a great deal of enthusiasm. A short time later he sent Kayserling this Air and Thirty Variations which was nicknamed *Goldberg Variations.*

Kayserling sent Bach a snuff box filled with a great deal of money as a token of his appreciation.

THE HARMONIOUS BLACKSMITH

Air and Variations for Harpsichord
(from Suite No. 5)

George Frederic Handel

There are two different stories as to why the nickname *Harmonious Blacksmith* has been given to this piece.

The first story is that one day, when Handel was in the town of Edgware, England, he heard a blacksmith whistling a tune. He was so impressed with the tune, that when he was composing this set of variations he remembered it and used it as his theme. This is the story a man called Richard Clark used in a book that he wrote about Handel in 1836. Mr. Clark also said that he had found the "actual" anvil used by the blacksmith and a monument which had been erected to the "actual" blacksmith.

The second story is probably the accurate one.

The original publisher of Handel's music was a music seller at Bath, England, named Mr. Linturn. When Mr. Linturn was a young man, he was taught to be a blacksmith, but when he became a little older, he decided to make his living from music. One of his favorite compositions was this particular Air and Variations. Mr. Linturn learned to play it so well that he was constantly asked to perform it.

One day Mr. Linturn had an idea. Instead of publishing this piece as every other piece was published, in a large volume, he would publish it separately. He would give it an imaginative nickname that would capture people's attention. The name he chose was *Harmonious Blacksmith.* His idea proved to be a good one. In this form the piece sold many more copies than it would have otherwise, and even today, many, many years later, everyone calls it by the nickname he gave it.

THE HUNT
Symphony No. 73 in D Major
JOSEPH HAYDN

During the time of Haydn, a hunt was a very festive and colorful occasion. Men in bright costumes, with their hunting dogs beside them, waited for the horn call which would announce the opening of the chase.

In 1780 Haydn wrote an opera, *La Fedalta Premiato* which was first performed at Esterháza. For the prelude to Act III, Haydn composed music that described just such a scene, called *La Chasse* (*The Hunt*). The oboes and horns are used in rhythmic tunes, calling the hunters to the chase. Haydn was so fond of this music that when he was composing his Symphony No. 73, he used the opera prelude for the last movement of the symphony. Because of this, he called the symphony, *The Hunt*.

ITALIAN SYMPHONY

Symphony No. 4 in A Major, Op. 90

FELIX MENDELSSOHN

Felix Mendelssohn visited Italy in 1830. While he was there, he spent much time watching the young people dance. His great favorite, the salterello, was a popular Roman dance performed by one or two persons, usually a man and a woman. The woman holds up her apron throughout the dance, and the dance is quick and hopping. The music is most often in a minor key and is played on a guitar or mandolin with tambourine accompaniment.

One evening, while Mendelssohn was watching the dancing of the salterello in front of the inn at Amalfi, he called out "Oh, that melody, mark it well, you shall find it again in some shape or form in a work of mine."

In the last movement of Mendelssohn's Fourth Symphony, there are two salterello themes. In each one the jumping or hopping step is very clear. It is because of this that Mendelssohn nicknamed the symphony *Italian Symphony*.

JUPITER

Symphony in C Major, K. 551

Wolfgang Amadeus Mozart

Sometimes it is difficult to know why certain nicknames are given to musical compositions. No one seems to know for certain why or from whom the symphony *Jupiter* received its nickname. Some believe that the English pianist and publisher, J. B. Cramer, was responsible for it. He described the symphony as "Godlike."

Jupiter was the supreme god of the ancient Romans. He was really the god of the heavens. His weapon was the thunderbolt. Perhaps the loud opening chords of the first movement of this symphony made Mr. Cramer think that Jove, himself, was hurling thunderbolts from the heavens, and the name *Jupiter* seemed appropriate.

LINZ SYMPHONY

Symphony in C Major, K. 425

Wolfgang Amadeus Mozart

Mozart was a great genius and many stories are told of how quickly he could write music. The story about the *Linz Symphony* is certainly one of the best.

Mozart was travelling home from Salzburg to Vienna. On his way he stopped in the city of Linz to give a concert. In a letter to his father, dated October 31, 1783, he wrote the following: "On Tuesday, November 4, I am giving a concert in the theater here, and as I have not a single symphony with me, I am writing a new one at breakneck speed which must be finished by that time."

It is hard to believe, but it is true: a brilliant, festive symphony was composed, written down, rehearsed, and performed within five days; it has since lived for almost two hundred years.

MILITARY POLONAISE

Polonaise for Piano in A Major, Op. 40 No. 1

FREDERIC CHOPIN

In the time of Chopin, the polonaise was the opening dance at the State Balls of the Polish Court. The polonaise is a stately, rhythmic dance, almost like a grand march.

Imagine a ball of great splendor. The men are in full military uniform, and the young ladies are wearing their most beautiful gowns. Partners are chosen, and the music begins. The young people dance the steps in their best fashion, because Chopin's music inspires them.

It was the particularly noble and martial character of this Polonaise, composed in Paris in 1838, that gave it the nickname *Military Polonaise*.

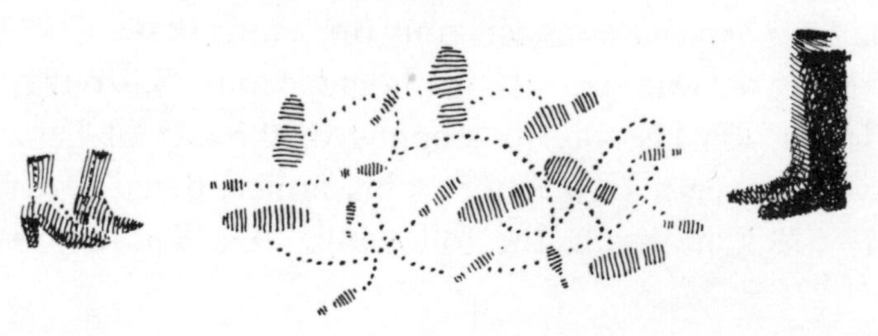

MINUTE WALTZ

Waltz for Piano in D♭ Major, Op. 64 No. 1

FREDERIC CHOPIN

This famous waltz really has two nicknames. Sometimes it is called *Minute Waltz* and other times it is called *Dog Waltz.*

The nickname *Minute Waltz* is not really an exact one. It takes at least one and a half minutes to play this piece so that it sounds well. However, the nickname has been the cause of several rather amusing stories. One of the famous ones is about two pianists attending a concert in New York City's Carnegie Hall. One of the pieces on the program was the *Minute Waltz.* When the performer had finished playing it, one pianist said to the other, "You know, this was the dullest quarter of an hour that I have ever spent."

The other nickname *Dog Waltz* was supposed to have been inspired by George Sand's dog. One evening while Chopin was sitting at the piano improvising, the little dog was running round and round, trying to catch his own tail. Chopin immediately composed this waltz, making the music go round and round, too.

THE MIRACLE

Symphony No. 96 in D Major

JOSEPH HAYDN

When this symphony was performed for the first time, there were many people in the audience. Haydn was there, too. After the orchestra had finished playing it, everyone rushed forward to get a better look at the great composer. In doing this, they left one place in the center of the concert room completely empty. Directly above this spot was a tremendous chandelier hanging from the ceiling. No sooner had the people moved than the chandelier crashed to the floor. There were cries of "A Miracle! A Miracle!" because no one had been killed or even hurt by the accident. Ever since that time this symphony has been known by its nickname, *The Miracle*.

MOONLIGHT SONATA

Sonata for Piano in C♯ Minor, Op. 27 No. 2

LUDWIG VAN BEETHOVEN

This is one of Beethoven's most popular sonatas. The first movement is particularly lovely and romantic. When one listens, one understands how the nickname could have been given, although the stories about the nickname are questionable.

There have been a number of different stories; here

are two of them:

1. Some say Beethoven composed the sonata in C♯ Minor when he was in love with his pupil, Giuletta Cuicciardi. As romance and moonlight go together, the nickname *Moonlight* seemed most appropriate. Unfortunately, it has been discovered that the real reason for Beethoven's dedicating this sonata to Giuletta Cuicciardi was not a romantic one. Beethoven had given her a Rondo in G and he wanted it back. The sonata was given to her in exchange for the rondo!

2. Others have said that a music critic of Beethoven's time, a man named Rellstab, nicknamed this sonata *Moonlight*. He compared the first movement of the work to a boat wandering on the Lake of Lucerne. He felt that Beethoven must have been on this lake when he was inspired to write the piece. The only trouble with this story is that Beethoven never visited the Lake of Lucerne.

A MUSICAL JOKE

Divertimento in F Major, K. 522

Wolfgang Amadeus Mozart

Mozart loved to make jokes. However, when he wrote this piece it was the first time that he had used his wit to twist music around.

First he wrote an opening melody which was very choppy and ended a bar too soon. His music is usually smooth and lovely. There are many wrong chords, which are never heard in Mozart's works. And he even wrote incorrectly for the instruments. The notes for the horn don't blend with the notes for the strings. The piece is full of humorous effects.

This was Mozart's way of poking fun at composers who were not very skillful in their music. Perhaps he was even trying to give the impression of how good music would sound if it were played by a poor village band. It really is a *Musical Joke*.

OX MINUET

Minuet for Orchestra

JOSEPH HAYDN

About this minuet a most amusing story is told. Haydn was such a kind man that it most likely is true.

One day a butcher called on Haydn. After giving him many compliments, he told him the real reason for his visit. His daughter was soon to be married. Her greatest wish was to have Haydn compose a piece of music especially for this occasion. Nothing would make her happier! Haydn was touched by this, and he told the butcher to come back the next day. When the butcher returned, a beautiful minuet was ready. The butcher thanked Haydn many times and left. Haydn thought the incident was over, but he was mistaken.

A few days later Haydn heard the music of his minuet being played outside his window. As he looked out, he was surprised to see a huge ox with gilded horns and wonderful decorations. All around the ox was a street orchestra playing the music of the minuet. The butcher went up to Haydn and said, "Dear sir, I thought that a butcher could not express his gratitude in a more becoming manner than by offering you the finest ox in his possession."

PASTORALE

Symphony No. 6 in F Major, Op. 68

LUDWIG VAN BEETHOVEN

Beethoven loved to take long walks in the country. We can imagine him dreaming away lazy hours lingering in the woods or by a stream. Perhaps he was resting and remembering back to such a day when the gentle, beautiful themes of this symphony came to his mind.

In the original score we have in Beethoven's own handwriting "6th Symphony by Ludwig van Beethoven 'The cheerful feelings which arise in man on arriving in the country.' "

When the Sixth Symphony was first performed in 1808, it was described on the program in the following manner:

"First piece:
  Pleasant feelings which awake in man on arriving in the country.
Second piece:
  Scene by the brook.
Third piece:
  Happy gathering of the country folk.
Fourth piece:
  Thunder and storm.
Fifth piece:
  Feelings of thanks to God after the storm."

When you listen to this symphony, listen for the sounds of nature that are imitated by different instruments in the orchestra. The strings imitate the brook. The low double basses sound like the coming of the storm. The flute sings the song of the nightingale. The oboe tries to sound very much like the song of the quail, and the clarinet imitates the cuckoo.

Beethoven really gives us a picture of a whole day in the country.

PATHETIQUE

Sonata for Piano in C Minor, Op. 13

LUDWIG VAN BEETHOVEN

When Beethoven was only twenty-eight years old, a terrible thing happened. He began to grow deaf. Soon he would not be able to hear the music that he composed.

At first Beethoven would not see anyone. He would not even write music. He thought that deafness was a shameful disease. Finally, because he was such a strong person, he conquered his feelings and worked harder than ever at his music.

Some of the most wonderful music came from this tragic period of Beethoven's life. The *Pathetique Sonata* was one of them.

The first movement of the sonata begins with a sad introduction and, even though the music changes to a faster tempo, the slow sad part keeps coming back. The second movement is also a slow one; and the third movement, although it is rather fast, still has a touch of sadness.

PATHETIQUE

Symphony No. 6 in B Minor

PETER ILICH TCHAIKOWSKY

Tchaikowsky could not make up his mind what name to give to his Sixth Symphony. First he thought of calling it *A Program Symphony,* but that did not please him. On the day the symphony was to have its first public performance, there was still no name for it. The concert program just listed it as Symphony No. 6.

The morning after the first performance, Tchaikowsky's brother, Modeste, found the composer up very early sitting at the tea table with the manuscript of the symphony in his hand. He was still trying to think of a name beside Symphony No. 6. Modeste suggested the word *Tragic* but Peter shook his head. As Modeste left the room, his brother was still undecided. He was getting more and more upset.

Suddenly Modeste reappeared at the door. *Pathetique* he called out.

"Perfect," cried Peter. "Bravo, *Pathetique!*" He wrote that word on the score, and it has become one of the most famous nicknames in music.

It is easy to understand why Tchaikowsky was so pleased with the name *Pathetique*; there is a feeling of sadness throughout the whole symphony. Even though the second movement is a gay waltz, the trio part of the movement has a drum beat which gives the effect of "the sound of fate." The symphony ends with an unusual movement, an *adagio lamentoso* (slow and sad).

THE RAGE OVER THE LOST PENNY

Rondo a Capriccio for Piano in G Major, Op. 129

LUDWIG VAN BEETHOVEN

Beethoven wrote this piece when he was quite young. Somehow the manuscript was mislaid and it was not until 1828, a year after Beethoven had died, that a copy was found and it was published. And not until 1947 was the original autographed copy belonging to Beethoven found, and then in the United States. On it Beethoven had written in German a title which, translated, says *Anger at the loss of a penny, abated in a Caprice.*

It is a humorous piece, full of surprises. The music suddenly gets loud because Beethoven is angry and stamps his foot. He can't find the penny! Then he decides to give up the search. The music gets soft and calm. When he starts the search all over again, you can almost see the music papers flying helter-skelter from the table. Finally, he gives up the search, and the piece ends calmly. His rage is exhausted.

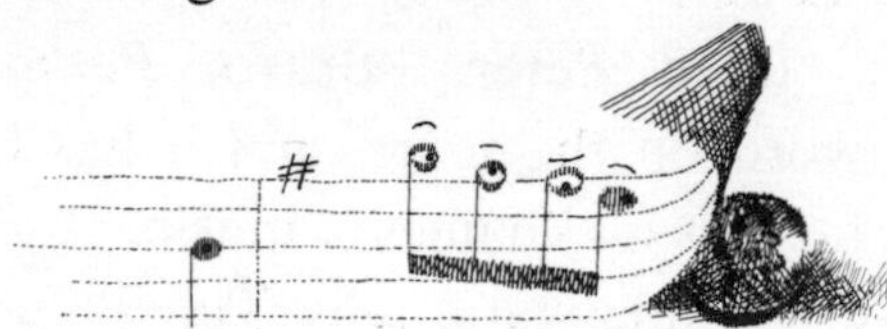

The great composer Robert Schumann imagined Beethoven saying while he was composing this piece, "Today I feel altogether unbuttoned," (This was an expression Beethoven used when he felt very merry); and then laughing like a lion, for he was always untamable, and adding "but with this capriccio I'll get you."

RAINDROP PRELUDE

Prelude No. 15 for Piano in D♭ Major

FREDERIC CHOPIN

On the island of Majorca there was a place called the Monastery of Valdemoso. When Chopin was composing a set of twenty-four preludes for the piano, he was living there with his friend, George Sand, and her family. On the day he was writing this particular prelude, Number 15 of the set, the rain was falling gently on the roof. George Sand felt that even though Chopin didn't realize it, the rain had inspired him to compose as he did and persuaded him to call it *The Raindrop Prelude.*

When you listen to this beautiful little piece, you will hear the gentle dripping of the rain on the roof of Valdemoso.

RAZOR QUARTET

String Quartet in F Minor, Op. 55 No. 2

JOSEPH HAYDN

Once An English publisher named John Bland came to visit Haydn at Esterháza. Bland was anxious to get the right to publish some of the master's new works.

One morning while Haydn was shaving himself, apparently with a very dull razor, Bland heard him exclaim, "I would give my best quartet for a good razor!" Bland rushed to his room, seized his own very good set of razors, and brought them to Haydn. Haydn was delighted and kept his promise. He gave Bland the manuscript for this quartet. It is one of Haydn's best, an excellent bargain for Bland to have received in exchange for a set of razors!

REVOLUTIONARY ÉTUDE

Étude for Piano in C Minor, Op. 10 No. 12

FREDERIC CHOPIN

When Chopin was in Stuttgart, Germany, in 1831, he heard that the Russians had conquered his beloved city, Warsaw. He was sad and upset by this news. The only way he could express his feelings was to compose a piece of music.

All through this brilliant étude, the left hand thunders with excitement. You can imagine armies storming the city. The strong melody of the right hand seems to be crying out in anguish. Not only is this piece known by its nickname *Revolutionary Étude,* but some people call it by still another nickname *The Fall of Warsaw*.

SPINNING SONG

Piano Piece, Op. 67 No. 4 in C Major, from Songs Without Words

FELIX MENDELSSOHN

Felix Mendelssohn composed a book of forty-nine pieces for the piano called *Songs Without Words.* Many of these pieces were given nicknames by the pianist and composer, Stephen Heller, who lived at the same time as Mendelssohn.

It is clear why Heller chose the nickname *Spinning Song* for this piece. The right hand plays two different parts at the same time. The lower part weaves round and round like a spinning wheel. The upper part has a singing melody, which sounds as though someone were singing while the wheel was turning.

SURPRISE SYMPHONY
Symphony No. 94 in G Major
JOSEPH HAYDN

Watching audiences, Haydn noticed that during the fast movements of his symphonies, most of the people kept at least one eye open. During the slow movements, however, almost everyone fell asleep. Because Haydn was fond of a joke, he decided to play a musical joke on his audiences just to see what would happen.

In the softest part of the slow movement of this symphony, when he knew that the audience would have fallen into its first snooze, there is a sudden bang from the full orchestra. Just as Haydn had anticipated, when it was played, everyone sat up in great surprise. Haydn laughed with glee. His joke had worked, and his symphony was nicknamed *Surprise Symphony*.

TOY SYMPHONY

Symphony in C Major

Joseph Haydn

In the year 1788, there was a great fair in the Bavarian town of Berchtesgaden. While visiting the fair, Haydn purchased seven toy instruments. They were a cuckoo, a trumpet, a whistle, a triangle, a quail, a rachet, and a drum.

Haydn was always a great joker. In one of his impish moments, he dashed off a little symphony in three movements. The last movement is played three times over, faster and faster each time. He wrote the music mostly for the toy instruments that he had bought at the fair. The only real musical instruments in the work are two violins and a double bass.

As soon as the symphony was finished, Haydn called his men to an important rehearsal. When the orchestra men found that they were expected to play a new symphony on toy instruments, they laughed so hard they could hardly play.

This *Toy Symphony* is still played, and people still laugh when they hear it. However, some recent musicians think Haydn may not have even written this symphony, that Leopold Mozart, Wolfgang's father, was the composer.

UNFINISHED SYMPHONY
Symphony No. 8 in B Minor
FRANZ SCHUBERT

There was once in the little Austrian town of Graz a music society called the Worthy Music Society. At one of the meetings of this group, two friends of Schubert suggested that the composer should be made an honorary member of the Society. Everyone agreed, and a letter was sent to Schubert in Vienna.

This was Schubert's modest answer: "I thank you most heartily for the certificate of honorary membership which you have so kindly sent me, and which, because of a long absence from Vienna, I only received a few days ago. May my ardor for music be so successful that some day I shall be completely worthy of this distinction. That I may also express my lively thanks in tones, I shall take the liberty to send your society as soon as possible one of my symphonies in score."

The score which he "took the liberty of sending" consisted of the two movements, and the nine measures of a third, of the famous *Unfinished Symphony*.

Somehow the score was mislaid. Years later an orchestra conductor, Herbeck, visited one of Schubert's old friends. As they were looking over yellowing manuscripts in his dusty workroom, the friend said, "Oh, I have still a lot of things of Schubert." He pulled out a mass of papers from an old-fashioned chest. Among them was this symphony, the *Unfinished,* which he gave to Herbeck.

Needless to say, Herbeck was delighted to have the

score. He conducted the first performance of the symphony at a concert of the Society of the Friends of Music, in Vienna on December 17, 1865. More than forty years had passed since Schubert composed it.

Why Schubert never finished this symphony has always been a mystery. It was not his last work because he did not die until six years after it was written. Perhaps he felt that in the two movements he had said all that he wanted to say.

Many years later, when a music critic wrote about this composition, he said: "Let us be thankful that Schubert never finished the work. Possibly the lost arms of Venus de Milo might disappoint if they were found and restored."

We also have to be thankful to Schubert's old friend for finding the score. Without him, we never would have been able to hear this music.

WATER MUSIC

Suite for Orchestra

George Frederic Handel

Before George I became King of England, he ruled Hanover, Germany. In Hanover, Handel served him as Capellmeister. However, Handel left this position to go and live in England.

King George was angry when Handel left, and he was still angry when he, himself, moved to England. Handel wanted to stay in England, but his chances of making a living were small without the King's favor.

Fortunately for Handel, he had two friends at Court, Lord Burlington and Baron Kilmansegg. They worked out a scheme that brought Handel back into the good graces of the King.

There was a royal water party on the river Thames. It was arranged that the King's barge was followed by another barge, containing Handel and a group of musicians. As they floated along, the musicians began to play a suite that Handel had composed especially for the occasion. The King liked the music so much that he wanted to know the name of the composer. When he heard that it was Handel, the composer was taken back into favor immediately.

Whether this story is true or not, we do not know; But we do know that just at this time the King gave Handel 200 pounds a year as a pension. We also know that when the King went on a journey to Hanover in 1716, he asked Handel to accompany him.

WITH TWO EYEGLASSES, OBLIGATO

Duet for Viola and 'Cello in E♭ Major

LUDWIG VAN BEETHOVEN

Not until the year 1912 was the composition *With Two Eyeglasses, Obligato* discovered and published.

Fritz Stein, a music editor, found it in a large collection of Beethoven's sketchbooks, which the composer kept from his fourteenth to his thirtieth years. These particular sketchbooks were in the British Museum in London, because the British Museum had bought them in 1875.

Why Beethoven scribbled the amusing name *With Two Eyeglasses, Obligato* on the piece has always been a puzzle. We know that Beethoven composed the duet for two friends, a 'cellist called Von Zneskell, and a violist. No one knows who the violist was or whether either of the men wore glasses.

Of course, there is the possibility that both the violist and 'cellist were nearsighted and had to wear glasses. But it is also possible that Beethoven felt that this music was so difficult that his friends would have to put on glasses before attempting to play it.

Whether or not the mystery of the name is ever solved doesn't matter, because the music is clear, powerful, and a joy to hear.

Stories OF MEN

Domenico Scarlatti

1685—1757

The year 1685 was a lucky one for music. In that year three of the greatest composers of all times were born. Domenico Scarlatti was born in Naples, Italy on October 26; Johann Sebastian Bach was born in Eisenach, Germany on February 23; and George Frederic Handel was born in Halle, Germany on March 21.

"Mimo," as Domenico was called, was the sixth of a family of ten children. Allesandro, Mimo's father, was an important composer of operas. He composed 115 of them. Much of the rehearsing for Allesandro's operas was done at home where Mimo could listen.

It is not exactly known who Mimo's first teacher of music was. He probably had lessons from some member of his family, but it is also possible that he just imitated what he heard. There is no record of his having received instruction at school either. However, when he reached his early teens it is known that he had regular lessons with his father on the organ, the harpsichord, and in composition. In a short time he became his father's prize pupil.

When Domenico was not quite sixteen, he was given his first position as a professional musician. He became the organist and composer for the royal chapel in Naples. He worked for six months and then asked for a leave because he wanted to go with his father on a trip to Rome and Florence. The leave was granted, and father and son set out for Rome.

In Rome, Domenico met some of his father's musical friends. In Florence he wrote his first known composition, a cantata. A *cantata* is a piece for chorus and soloists in several movements that includes primarily arias, duets, and chorales. The singing is usually accompanied by instruments. Although this composition was never published, the manuscript can be seen in the Conservatory of Music in Parma, Italy.

After Domenico's ten months' leave was up, he returned to Naples. Now, beside his work at the royal chapel, he also began composing operas. He wrote two of them before he was eighteen. One of them, *Il Giustino,* was performed in Naples in what was really a family affair. Domenico's uncle Tommaso was a popular comic tenor, and he sang the leading part; another uncle painted the scenery; and a third uncle was the producer of the opera. Several arias of *Il Giustino* are still in existence, but they are not considered very good examples of Domenico's music.

Soon after this Domenico's father decided that it would be best for his son to go to Venice. In that city there were many opera houses, and the young man would find more opportunities to have his work performed. Domenico found Venice all his father had hoped it would be. Best of all, to him, was the stimulation of being with other musicians. Masquerade parties were fashionable in Venice just then, and he was often invited, as were other musicians. At one of them, once, he had just arrived when he heard some beautiful harpsichord playing. He walked over to the instrument, but the gentleman who was playing was wearing a mask and it was impossible to tell who he was. In a loud voice Domenico exclaimed, "This can be no one but the famous Saxon or the Devil!" The man was Handel, "the famous Saxon." After that Handel and Scarlatti became good friends.

The following year a Cardinal Ottoboni, who often helped young musicians, became interested in Scarlatti. Handel was already well known to the musical public of Venice, and in order to show that Scarlatti, too, was a gifted young man, Cardinal Ottoboni arranged a contest between the two. An audience and judges were invited to the Cardinal's palace to hear Handel and Scarlatti play the organ and the harpsichord. They both played so well that it was difficult to decide who should be the winner. Finally, Handel was chosen as the best organist and Scarlatti as the best harpsichordist.

From Venice, Scarlatti went to Rome. There he was given the position of opera composer for the private theater of the Polish Queen, Marie, who was living in Rome. One of the best known operas that Scarlatti composed for the Queen was *Tolomeo*. This opera was thought to be lost, but the first act has recently been discovered in an old bookshop in Rome.

Unfortunately, the Queen was very extravagant; she

was soon left without money, and could not pay Domenico for his work. He had to find another position, and in a short while he was appointed musical director of St. Peters. At the Vatican, he conducted the choir, played the organ, and composed a great deal of choral music. Most of this music has also been lost. It is thought that Domenico took it with him when he went to Portugal in 1719 as chapel master to King João V, and it was lost there.

In Portugal, beside his duties as chapel master, Scarlatti gave harpsichord lessons to the King's daughter, Maria Barbara. Maria Barbara became a fine harpsichordist and was a devoted pupil. She did much to help her teacher; and some years later when she became Queen of Spain, she took Scarlatti and his family to Spain with her.

We do not know too much about Domenico's personal life. He did not leave any letters and there were no anecdotes written about him. We do know that he married for the first time when he was forty-three years old. He married a beautiful young girl of sixteen named Catalina, and they went to Spain to be near Scarlatti's pupil, Maria Barbara, who was now Queen of Spain.

Catalina and Domenico had five children, three girls and two boys. It was a happy marriage, but unfortunately Catalina died quite suddenly at the early age of twenty-six. Domenico was lonely after Catalina's death and two years later, in 1740, he married a Spanish girl named Anastasia. There were four children, two girls and two boys, born of this marriage. Not one of Scarlatti's nine children was a musician.

The development of Scarlatti's music is much easier to trace. During his early years he wrote mostly operas and cantatas. Domenico was devoted to his father. He thought that everything his father did was wonderful, and as a young man he even imitated his father's compositions. It was only after his father's death in 1725 that he really began to do original things. His great works were not operas like his father's, but compositions for the harpsichord, most of them sonatas.

Scarlatti invented his own way of writing a sonata. His are always in one movement and are very original. Most of the very first pieces of music that can at all be considered sonatas, and not just dance movements, were written by him.

During Scarlatti's years in Spain, he composed many beautiful sonatas for the Queen. You can hear the influence of Spanish music when you listen to these pieces. There are sounds like the click of castanets, the strumming of guitars, and the noises of gay village bands cleverly woven into the music. When he was fifty-three years old, thirty of these sonatas were published under the title *Essercize*. This was the most important work Scarlatti had published up until this time. At the end of the *Essercize* there is a piece now called *The Cat's Fugue*. This nickname was given to it at the beginning of the 1800's and on the cover of an old copy is a picture of four cats around a piano.

This is the theme that the pussycat was supposed to have "played":

In other sonatas, Scarlatti wrote, besides fast scales and arpeggios, many parts for crossed hands. The left hand crossed over the right hand, or sometimes the other way around. When Scarlatti got older and fatter, it is said that it was a funny sight to see him trying to cross his hands.

Here are a few measures of a part for crossed hands:

As the years went by, Scarlatti wrote sonata after sonata. These compositions are so brilliant that composers like Mendelssohn, Chopin and Liszt, who wrote a hundred years later, were helped by studying them.

Scarlatti's fame as a composer travelled to England and even to America. It is said that a young man in Virginia wrote to his brother in England, asking him to send "Scarlatti for the Harpsichord."

When this important composer died in Spain at the age of seventy-two, he left his large family, many debts, and over six hundred compositions. Scarlatti's last composition, *Salve Regina,* was not for harpsichord but for a soprano and stringed instruments. In it, we hear his prayer to the Virgin Mary.

The manuscripts of Scarlatti's music were scattered everywhere. It was not until 1910 that an Italian named Allesandro Longo undertook to collect all the works available and make them into a fine edition. Most of the sonatas are now played on the piano, but there are still people who prefer to play them on the harpsichord.

George Frederic Handel

1685—1759

Georg Friedrich Händel was born in Halle, Germany, on February 23, 1685. During his lifetime he spent many years in England and became an English citizen. It is because of this that his name is almost always spelled in the English fashion, George Frederic Handel.

George Frederic's father was an elderly gentleman of 63 when his son was born. The father was a man who knew what he wanted, and he was determined that his boy should have a profession much higher than his own. Handel's father was a barber-surgeon. Of course, in those days a barber did more than just cut hair. He performed minor operations and sometimes even pulled a tooth. But this was not to be for George Frederic. He was to be a famous lawyer.

Since he was so determined that his son should be a lawyer, Dr. Handel was unhappy when he discovered that George Frederic loved music and wanted to be a musician. To Dr. Handel, this was much worse than being a barber. He forbade his son to study music, saying, "Music is something you should enjoy but not make a profession of."

Fortunately for young Handel, his mother and his favorite aunt, *Tante* Anna, loved music and helped him secretly. Aunt Anna, who lived with the Handels, thought of a scheme whereby a clavichord was smuggled into the attic. The walls and floor of this room were made of heavy timber, and Anna thought that it would be difficult for the sounds to go through the house. George Frederic was careful, however, and although he practiced for hours and hours, it was always when his father was not at home. One day Handel's father arrived home earlier than usual. He heard the sounds of a clavichord and was puzzled. Where was the music coming from? Finally he traced the sounds to the attic. At first, when he saw George at the clavichord, he was upset. "The clavichord will have to be taken away," he said. But when he saw the look of sadness on his son's face, he could only change his mind. George Frederic was permitted to keep his instrument.

One morning soon after this incident, Handel's father had to go to the Court of Saxe-Weissenfels to see some of his patients. Handel, who was still just a boy of seven, begged to go along. He had heard that there was beautiful music at the court, and he wanted to hear it; but his father said, "Oh, no, my son, you will come some other time." The story is that Handel wanted so much to go that he ran after his father's coach. He ran and ran until he was so exhausted he almost gave up. Fortunately for him, the horses stopped to rest, and George Frederic called out with all his might, "Father, father, it is I, George Frederic." Doctor Handel could hardly believe his eyes when he saw his son. He knew at once that there was nothing to do but take the boy along.

This trip was the greatest thing that could have happened to George Frederic. He was permitted to play the organ at the court, and when the Duke heard how beautifully he played, he said, "This child has extraordinary gifts; he must be trained." Handel's father tried to explain that he wanted his son to become a great lawyer, but the Duke insisted that George Frederic study music. Dr. Handel did not dare disobey because if he did, he might lose his position at court.

When George Frederic came back to Halle, he was accepted by the organist Zachau as a pupil. Besides the organ, the boy learned to play the harpsichord, the violin, the oboe and to compose music. After three years of hard work Zachau said, "The boy knows more than I do, he must be sent to Berlin."

In Berlin, George Frederic was called "The Wonder Child." Unfortunately, he had been there only a short time when he was called back to Halle because his father was dying. Old Mr. Handel still had not forgotten his early dreams, and before his death he made George Frederic promise to continue his law studies as well as his music.

A short time later George Frederic entered the university in Halle and at the same time accepted the position of organist at the *Domkirche*. *Kirche* is the German word for church. In this way he kept his promise to his father and was also able to earn money for his mother and himself. But as hard as he tried, he could not put his heart into his law studies. Finally, after much thought, and with the permission of his mother, he left the university to give all his time to music.

Handel wanted to go to Hamburg because that city was a much larger one than Halle and he was sure that he would have many more opportunities for his work. He bid his mother and his Aunt Anna goodbye and set out to seek his fortune.

He was only in Hamburg a few days before he got a position playing the violin and the harpsichord at the Opera House. It was here that Handel met a musician named Johann Matheson. At first the two were friendly, but when Matheson realized how well Handel played the harpsichord, he became very jealous. Once during a performance Matheson challenged Handel to a duel because Handel would not let him play the harpsichord. After the performance the two young men met in the courtyard. Fortunately the point of Matheson's sword broke on a metal button of Handel's waistcoat.

During the remainder of Handel's stay in Hamburg he worked very hard at his compositions. His first opera *Almira* was performed there when he was only twenty years old.

Handel's next dream was to go to Italy, because there he could learn more about opera than he could anywhere else in the world. Handel arrived in Italy when he was twenty-one years old. He visited Florence, Rome, Venice and Naples. He learned much, and during his lifetime he composed forty operas. These made him famous in his day, but in our time they are not considered his most important works. The melody of one of the songs in his opera *Xerxes* is still very popular. It is known as Handel's *Largo* and has been arranged for many instruments. Here are a few measures of the beautiful melody:

After three years in Italy, Handel became homesick for Germany. When he went back to Germany, he met George, Elector of Hanover, who persuaded him to accept the position of *Capellmeister,* director of music, at his court. Handel agreed to take the position only if he could first go to England. The Elector gave his permission, and off to England Handel went.

Handel loved England; and the English people loved him and his music; so he decided to stay. He did nothing about returning to the job of capellmeister. After he had been in England for quite a while, the very same Elector, George of Hanover, became George II of England. The Elector was still furious with Handel because he had remained away from Hanover. It was only a clever scheme carried out by two of Handel's good friends that made the King forgive him.

During one of Handel's visits to his mother in Halle, he just missed meeting Johann Sebastian Bach. When Bach heard that Handel was in Halle, he walked twenty-five miles in the hope of meeting his fellow composer. He arrived at the home of Handel's mother just after Handel had gone. She could only say, "You have come all the way from Leipzig to see our Handel, and just a few minutes ago did he leave in his coach." These two great men, although born in the same year and in the same country, never did meet.

Handel's fame in England grew and grew. He was the greatest oratorio composer that that country had ever had. An *oratorio* is a long work for vocal soloists, chorus and orchestra, and is usually written around a religious theme. It tells a story, but it is performed without scenery or costumes. The first oratorio Handel wrote was *Esther,* and the last one was *Jeptha.* The *Messiah* is perhaps the best known and the greatest of all of them. It is still performed all over the world at Christmas time. It is said that this great work, which took Handel only twenty-four days to write, is the work of an "inspired giant." Handel was living in a dream world when he composed this music. He did not leave his house. His servant brought him food, but many times he did not even touch it. This was unusual because he loved food and ate a great deal. When Handel had finished writing Part II of the *Messiah,* which ends with the *Hallelujah Chorus,* his servant found him with tears streaming down his face. He said, "I did think I did see all Heaven before me, and the great God, Himself."

When King George II heard the *Hallelujah Chorus,* he was so moved that he sprang up to his feet and remained standing as long as the chorus sang. And still today when this work is performed, audiences all over the world stand and remain standing while the great chorus is sung. Here are a few measures of this music.

Another composition of Handel that is exciting, but not in the same way as the *Messiah,* is his suite *Music for the Royal Fireworks.*

To celebrate the signing of the Treaty of Aix La Chapelle (this was at the end of a war between England, France, and Holland) in October, 1748, King George II ordered great festivities. He sent for Handel and told him to compose special music for the occasion. The King also ordered an architect to design a high new building in London's Green Park. Fireworks were to be set off from the top of the building.

When everything was completed, a rehearsal was held for Handel's new composition. This music consisted of an overture and seven other pieces; it was played by one hundred musicians. Twelve thousand people attended the rehearsal.

On the day of the actual celebration, the crowd was even more tremendous. After the overture to Handel's suite was played, 101 cannons fired the royal salute. And then, as the fireworks were set off, panic broke loose. The top of the building had caught on fire! People ran in every direction. Several people lost their lives, and the building was completely destroyed. No one heard the rest of Handel's *Music for the Royal Fireworks* that day, but since then this music has been played by orchestras everywhere.

Besides *Music for the Royal Fireworks,* operas, oratorios, anthems, organ concertos, and music for wind instruments, Handel also wrote many pieces for the harpsichord. These are now played on the piano.

One of the most popular works in his collection of harpsichord music is the Air and Variations nicknamed *The Harmonious Blacksmith.* When a composer takes an air or a theme and changes it by "dressing it up in different costumes," this is called a variation. The theme is almost always easy to recognize.

Here is Handel's theme for *The Harmonious Blacksmith.*

As for Handel's personal life, very little is known. He left no diary and only a few polite letters. Although Handel is said to have had several romances, he never married. Somehow his love affairs did not last very long. Perhaps the saying "Handel's only real love was music" was a true one.

During the last eight years of Handel's life, he went completely blind. Even an operation by an important eye doctor did no good. In spite of this he kept on playing and conducting his works. His two good friends, a father and son, John and Christopher Smith, were a great help to him. The father was an old school friend from Halle whose name had been Johann Schmitt.

On April 6, 1759, Handel conducted a performance of the *Messiah.* At the very end of the work he fainted and had to be carried home. When he recovered a little he said, "I want to die on Good Friday in the hope of rejoining the good Lord." His wish was granted. He died on Good Friday, 1759, when he was seventy-four years old.

The English people were proud of their great Handel. He was buried in Westminster Abbey, where all the great and important people of England are buried.

Johann Sebastian Bach

1685—1750

On March 21, 1685, Johann Sebastian Bach, the greatest of all the Bachs, was born in Eisenach, Germany. It is said that in Eisenach "musical Bachs grew on every tree." For nearly two hundred years, members of Sebastian's family had been musicians. Some played the organ, some sang in church choirs, others composed music, and still others made clavichords and violins. The clavichord was the kind of a piano used in the days of Bach.

From the time that Sebastian was a tiny baby, he heard music being played in his home. His father, Johann Ambrosius, was a violin teacher and organist. When Sebastian was very young, his father gave him lessons on the violin. Everyone was amazed at how quickly Sebastian learned to get beautiful clear tones on his small violin.

Once each year all the Bachs got together to have a music festival. Each year Sebastian could hardly wait for that great day to arrive. There was music of every kind, but his particular delight was the quodlibet. A *quodlibet* is a humorous piece of music which includes snatches of well-known popular melodies. Several melodies are played at the same time by different players. There was a great deal of merry laughter at these amusing songs, and Sebastian was left with pleasant memories of happy times. Many years later when he wrote his *Goldberg Variations* for the harpsichord, he composed a quodlibet at the end of the thirtieth variation.

The happy days of childhood ended for Sebastian when he was not quite ten years old. His mother and father both died, and he went to live with his brother, Christoff. Christoff and his family lived in the village of Ohrdruff. Christoff was the organist at the church, and young Sebastian was invited to sing in the choir and to play on his violin. Christoff also taught Sebastian how to play the clavier. But he was not permitted by his brother to practice more than one hour a day. Nor was he allowed to play all of the difficult music his brother had. Christoff always said, "Oh no, you are not old enough for that music."

Sebastian knew that the book with the music that he wanted to play was locked in a bookcase in the downstairs room. One day, as he was staring at the book, he noticed that there was an open space just large enough for his hand to go through. That night when everyone was asleep, he crept downstairs, squeezed his hand through the opening, and carefully pulled the book out. Since he was not permitted to have a candle in his room, he copied as much of the music as he could by moonlight. He did this every night for six months, and finally the precious music was his.

Even when the music was his own, Sebastian was careful to play it only if his brother was not at home. But one day Christoff arrived unexpectedly and heard Sebastian playing the forbidden music. He was very angry. He rushed into the room and took the book away. Sebastian burst into tears, but Christoff would not return the book.

Soon after this, Sebastian decided to leave his brother's home. He wanted to be a musician and was determined to seek the training he needed. With a school friend, he started out on a journey of two hundred miles to the choir school at St. Michael's in Lüneberg. The boys had very little money between them and they had to walk the whole way. But this mattered little when they finally reached the school and to their great joy were accepted as pupils.

At Lüneberg Sebastian worked very hard at the organ, the clavier, and at his compositions. He was also able to earn some money singing in the choir. But money was scarce, and once he walked many miles to Hamburg to hear the great organist Adam Reinken play. On this journey he stopped to rest outside an inn just to smell the odors of food that were coming out of the kitchen. He had no money to buy food. Suddenly a window opened and two herring heads were thrown out. Sebastian picked them up and found in each a Danish ducat. He was overjoyed. There was money enough to buy some food and to come again to Hamburg to hear the great organist play.

Sebastian graduated from St. Michael's in 1702. He was then seventeen years old and had to find some way of earning a living. The sensible thing to do, he decided was to go to Thuringia, a province in central Europe. Some of his relatives were living there and he knew he could stay with them until he found a job.

Soon after Sebastian arrived in Thuringia, he went to work in the nearby village of Arnstadt. He was engaged as a violinist in the chamber orchestra of Johann Ernst.

Sebastian was not too happy fiddling away in a small orchestra and being treated like a servant. But he had to put up with these discomforts because he was given a place to live and a small salary besides. Most important of all, he had time to practice the organ, and Sebastian's ambition was to become an organist in a church.

The following year, when Sebastian was eighteen years old, he was invited to try out the new organ of the church in Arnstadt. Sebastian played so remarkably well that even though the church had a regular organist, he was immediately engaged as second organist.

However, Sebastian soon discovered that his position was more difficult than he had thought it would be. Besides playing the organ, he had to train the choir.

Some of the boys in the choir and some of the boys who played the accompanying instruments were older than he and took advantage of him. They were disrespectful and would not follow his instructions. Sebastian often lost his temper, and once he called the bassoon player "a nanny goat bassoonist." The bassoonist challenged Sebastian to a fight, and after the rehearsal the two young men met outside. Fortunately, some passers-by stopped the boys before the fight went too far. Since Sebastian carried a sword, the end might have been a sad one.

Although the situation in Arnstadt grew more and more unpleasant, Sebastian did not give up. He was helped by a friendship with his cousin Barbara. She was a fine girl and sympathetic to his problems. But she was also able to convince him that he must control his temper.

Finally, however, Sebastian felt that he needed a change, and he asked for a leave. It was given to him, and he went off to Lübeck to hear the great organist Buxtehude. Lübeck was 230 miles from Arnstadt, and Sebastian walked all the way. When he listened to the great master play, he forgot all about the long journey.

Buxtehude also listened to Sebastian play and was so impressed that he offered to give Sebastian his own position as soon as he retired. When Sebastian realized that to accept the offer he would have to marry Buxtehude's daughter, he refused. Barbara was waiting for him in Arnstadt!

Sebastian returned to Arnstadt in February, 1706. Inspired by Buxtehude's compositions, he composed some organ preludes of his own.

The following year Sebastian was offered the position of organist in Mühlhausen. He was happy about this for two reasons: he could leave Arnstadt; and he would earn more money and could ask Barbara to marry him. He did, and they were married on October 17, 1707. They left for Mühlhausen immediately.

In Mühlhausen, Sebastian had another disappointment. He was not permitted to play the kind of music he wanted to play. This he could not bear. As soon as his year's work was finished, he decided to look for another position.

It was the custom in the days of Bach for composers and musicians to be employed by royal and noble families. So Bach applied for a position at the Court of Duke Wilhelm Ernst in Weimar. The Duke was so impressed with Bach's organ playing, that not only did he offer him the position of chapel organist and chamber musician, but he doubled the salary that Bach had received in Mühlhausen.

A few months later Barbara and Sebastian set out for Weimar. The trip was an especially difficult one because Barbara was expecting a baby. Barbara and Sebastian finally arrived in Weimar and before long they were settled in their new home. Bach was happy in his position, and he was also happy because his first daughter Catherina was born in December of that year. (1708)

Besides working at the required duties of his new position, Bach worked very enthusiastically at his composition. It was in Weimar that Bach composed some of his greatest organ works.

Duke Wilhelm was generous to Bach. By 1717 his income was twice as much as it had been in 1708. The Bach family had also increased. There were now four children, and one of the boys, Carl Philipp Emanuel, was already one of his father's most enthusiastic pupils. Bach was never too busy to look after the musical education of his children.

Things went well in Weimar until the end of 1716. At that time Bach was disturbed because the Capellmeister to the Duke had died and this position, which was higher than the one held by Bach, was not given to him. Bach decided to look for work elsewhere. He soon was offered the position of Capellmeister to the Prince of Cöthen. Because Bach accepted this new position before his work in Weimar was finished, the Duke of Weimir put Bach in jail for one month. Barbara and the children went on to Cöthen, and Bach joined them as soon as the month was up.

Bach found his work in Cöthen most enjoyable, and he was happy to be with his family again. He began to teach his son Wilhelm Friedemann the clavier, and he even composed a special instruction book for him. On the title page of the book Bach wrote the following: "Little Clavier Book for Wilhelm Friedemann begun in Cöthen on January 22, 1720." It was also for Wilhelm Friedemann that Bach wrote the now well-known *Two and Three Part Inventions*. In Friedemann's book they were called *Inventionen und Sinfonienen* (The Two Part Inventions were called "Inventionen" and the Three Part Inventions "Sinfonienen").

An *invention* is a short piece with one theme which is worked out as a counterpoint exercise. That is: First the right hand plays the theme, then the left hand plays it. The hand that is waiting for its turn plays a counter theme. These inventions that Bach wrote for his son are still studied and played by musicians all over the world.

Here is the theme of the Two Part Invention Number Eight in F Major:

In the summer of 1720 Bach went away on a trip. When he returned to Cöthen, he found bad news awaiting him. His wife Barbara had suddenly taken ill and died within a few days. This was a terrible shock to Bach, and the following year was a most difficult one for him. No one knows how he managed to keep a family of seven children together and still do as much teaching and composing as he did. That year he composed about seventy-five works! Among these compositions are the six *Brandenburg Concertos.*

One of Bach's favorite pupils at this time was a young lady named Anna Magdalena. Teacher and pupil fell in love and were married on December 3, 1721. Together they had thirteen children, making twenty Bach children in all. Anna Magdalena was a most musical girl, and Bach wrote a special group of pieces for her called *Clavier Book for Anna Magdalena Bach.* These compositions are still played by many students today.

Here are a few measures of the one called *Musette:*

During Bach's stay in Cöthen, one of his greatest accomplishments was his composition called *The Well Tempered Clavichord.* This is a collection of forty-eight preludes and fugues for the clavier, written in every key. For instance, there is a Prelude and Fugue in C Major, in C Minor, in C♯ Major, in C♯ Minor, and so on.

In order to have the preludes and fugues sound the way Bach wanted them to, he invented a new system of fingering. He used the thumb which had seldom been used in clavier playing before.

The Well Tempered Clavichord is still studied and played by every serious musician. Here are a few measures of the theme of the second fugue, in C minor.

During his lifetime Bach wrote many fugues. A *fugue* is a composition in which there are several parts or voices. The whole is built on a melody called a *subject*. First the subject is announced by itself, and then it is imitated in the other voices one after the other. Whenever a new voice plays the subject, the other voices go on playing something else. Bach's melodies, or subjects, are the most beautiful in all music.

After Bach had been in Cöthen, which was a rather small town, for six years, he decided that he would like to live in a larger city. He was pleased when a position was offered to him in Leipzig, because Leipzig was a thriving city of 30,000.

Bach's remaining years were spent as the Cantor of Leipzig. He had the full responsibility for all of the music at the two large churches and at three of the smaller ones. During this time Bach composed 265 church cantatas alone. Among these are the *B Minor Mass,* the *St. Mathew Passion* and the *Christmas Oratorios.* He also composed popular or secular cantatas. One of the well-known ones is the *Coffee Cantata.*

Bach's great gift for improvisation was well-known. Once, when he was in the palace of Frederic the Great of Prussia, the King gave Bach a theme to improvise upon. Bach immediately played a three part fugue, using the King's theme as the subject. The King was so pleased that he asked Bach to play a fugue in six parts. This was difficult even for Bach, and Bach asked permission to take it home with him so that he could have more time to work on it.

Back in Leipzig, Bach not only wrote a six part fugue, but he also composed some other pieces and sent the whole set to the King with the following inscription: (Part of it)

"Most Gracious King!

In deepest humility I dedicate herewith to your Majesty a musical offering, the noblest part of which derives from your Majesty's Own August Hand"—

This set of pieces has always been known as *The Musical Offering.*

Another important work of Bach which dates from this time is the composition for clavier called *The Goldberg Variations.*

The very last composition of Bach is *The Art of The Fugue.* The great master became ill while he was composing this tremendous work, and the many pages of the manuscript were not all gathered together until two years after he died. His death came on July 28, 1750.

Besides being a great composer Bach was also a wonderful teacher. Some of his pupils, including his sons Wilhelm Friedemann and Philipp Emanuel, became distinguished musicians; but not one could compare with the genius of his teacher.

Of all the many compositions he wrote for organ, clavier, harpsichord, 'cello, violin, orchestra, and voices, only a few were published during his lifetime. In 1850, one hundred years after Bach's death, a group of German musicians got together and formed The Bach Gesellschaft. This was an organization that devoted itself to the publication of Bach's works. The first volume was published in 1851 and by 1900 sixty volumes had been published. This organization also built a Bach Museum at Eisenach in the house in which Bach was born.

Giuseppe Tartini

1692—1770

Giuseppe Tartini was born in Pirano, Istria, on April 8, 1692. Istria was a little country near Venice.

The Tartini family was not a musical one. Giuseppe's father was a successful business man, and the family lived in a beautiful villa called Struegnano. It was here that Giuseppe, his brothers, Domenico, Antonio, and Pietro, and a sister, who died when she was very young, were born.

Giuseppe's father was devoted to the church. His one great hope was that Giuseppe would grow up to be a priest. Therefore, Giuseppe was sent to the Seminary of Capo d'Istria where he could learn the things he needed to know. The few years that he spent at this school were unhappy ones. He disliked all his studies except his violin lessons. He did not want to be a priest. Finally, after much discussion, he convinced his father that he must choose another vocation. When his father asked him what he would like to be, he replied, "Father, if I must have a profession other than music, I would like to be a lawyer." So Giuseppe was enrolled in the University of Padua where he could prepare for the law.

Giuseppe was a good student, but he soon became restless. His new passion was fencing and he spent many hours away from school competing in fencing matches. In a short time he became known as the best swordsman in Padua. When Giuseppe's father heard of this, he sent for his son immediately.

"Young man," he said, in an angry tone, "what does this mean? You were sent to school to become a lawyer, not a swordsman." Giuseppe tried to convince his father that being a fencing master would bring him fame and fortune, but his father would not hear of it. Both father and son were stubborn, and when Giuseppe refused to give up his fencing, his father cancelled his monthly allowance.

At first Giuseppe thought this was a terrible thing, but it soon turned out to be the best thing that could possibly have happened. He went back to his music and discovered that he wanted to be a violinist more than anything else in the world. He practiced for hours and hours. In order to earn money he gave violin lessons. And he was such a good teacher that in a short time he had more pupils than he could handle.

One of Giuseppe's pupils was a beautiful girl named Elizabeth. It is thought that she was the niece of Cardinal Giorgo Cornari, Archbishop of Padua. The two young people fell in love, but they knew the Cardinal would never consent to their marriage. So they ran off and got married. The Cardinal was furious, just as they had thought he would be, and threatened to put Giuseppe in prison for marrying a girl of fifteen without her guardian's consent. Elizabeth grew alarmed and convinced her new husband that he must leave Padua immediately. During the night Giuseppe disguised himself as a priest and fled from the city.

The unhappy young man, just twenty, headed for Rome. It was quite a distance from Padua to Rome, and because he had very little money the travelling was hard. After a few days he became so weary that he was almost in despair. He did not know what to do next when finally good luck came his way. In one of the villages he met a relative who listened to his story and promised to help him. The relative was custodian at the monastery at Assissi, and it was to the monastery that he took Tartini.

The abbot at the monastery was very kind to Giuseppe. He was given food and lodging, and he stayed for almost two years. Not too much is known about his life at the monastery, except that it was a time of serious study. He worked hard on his violin and his compositions. Padre Boemo, the organist at the monastery, helped a great deal. He taught him counterpoint, which was valuable to him in his composing. Although each composer handles counterpoint in his own way, there are basic rules that almost all follow.

One of the most famous of Tartini's compositions was written in Assissi. It is the difficult violin sonata nicknamed *The Devil's Trill.* It is still studied and performed by violinists all over the world. Here are a few bars of this music:

Many people were attracted to the outside of the monastery by the beautiful sounds of Tartini's music as he practiced. The people begged for an opportunity to come in and listen. Padre Boemo asked Tartini if he would give some concerts for the congregation, and he agreed on one condition: he must play behind a screen so as not to be recognized. In all this time no one had discovered where he was hiding.

A series of concerts were given, and all went well. No one knew who the musician was. But then one day many people had come from all over Italy on a pilgrimage to the tomb of St. Francis in Assissi. When they passed the Monastery, they heard Tartini's violin playing, and some of them went in to listen. Suddenly, as the sweet sounds came from the unknown player, the screen in front of him blew down and there stood Tartini! Unfortunately, one member of the audience was a gentleman from Padua. He recognized Tartini at once, and as soon as he returned to Padua, he informed the Cardinal of his discovery. Elizabeth was overjoyed when she heard the news. She begged her uncle to let her husband come home, and he finally consented.

There was great joy in all the city when Tartini came back to Padua. He had become a wonderful violinist and was still remembered as a great teacher. As a fitting welcome, he was given a position at the famous Capella del Santo. This *capella,* or chapel, was one of the finest in all of Italy. It was an honor to have a position here because only the best singers and the best instrumentalists were engaged. He was also given permission to give concerts in other places.

The Chancellor of Bohemia, Count Kinsky, invited Tartini to come to Prague. He was to play at a festival concert in honor of the coronation of the Emperor Charles VI. Tartini's playing created such a sensation that he was asked to stay and play in the private orchestra of the Count. He did this for almost two years until he became so homesick that he had to return to Padua.

Back home again, Tartini started a school of violin playing known as The School of the Nations. The Master's reputation had travelled so far that students came from many countries to study with him. Tartini became known as "The Master of The Nations."

Many of the compositions Tartini wrote were written for his students. In these works he used new ideas which improved their playing. It is said that Tartini composed more pieces for the violin than anyone before or after him. He wrote about 200 concertos and as many sonatas. The concertos are for solo violin and orchestra, and the sonatas are either for violin alone or for violin and piano. He also wrote 50 variations on a theme of Corelli which is called *L'Arte dell Arco* or *The School of the Bow*. Arcangelo Corelli was an Italian violinist and composer who lived from 1653 until 1713.

Beside all these compositions which have been studied and played by violinists all over the world, Tartini wrote important articles, or treatises, on violin playing. Only a few years ago one of these, which was thought to be lost, was discovered in Italy and is now in the United States. The University of California purchased it for its music library.

Tartini was also very inventive. He improved the sound of the violin by making the strings thicker. The bow that the player draws across the violin is important, too, in the making of music. Tartini improved it by making it of lighter wood and by shaping the wood at the heel of the bow so that the violinist could get a surer grip on it.

In Padua, Tartini was greatly loved by young and old. When his health began to fail in 1768, everyone was sad. The last two years of his life were spent in much suffering, and only the presence of his faithful pupils soothed him a little.

After his death, Tartini's admirers erected a life-size statue of him that still stands in the Parato della Valle. It can be seen there today, as can his house, which is just as he left it.

Franz Joseph Haydn

1732—1809

The river Leitha flows through the little town of Rohrau in the eastern part of Austria. Franz Joseph Haydn was born in Rohrau in 1732. It is not certain whether the day was March 31 or April 1, but Sepperl, as the boy was called in the Austrian fashion, liked to say that it was March 31.

Sepperl was the second child of a family of twelve. His mother, Maria, had been a cook in the castle of Count Harrach, the local overlord. Mathias, Sepperl's father, was a wheelright, and he repaired all of Count Harrach's coaches. He had still another job and that was to go from house to house to settle boundary disputes and to see that the fences were repaired. Sepperl loved to trudge along with his father and amuse him by humming little tunes.

After a hard day's work Sepperl's father used to sit by the fireplace, with his family around him, and sing his favorite folk songs. He was especially proud because he could accompany the songs on a harp, which he had taught himself to play. Before long Sepperl joined in the singing, too. Everyone was amazed at how quickly he learned the songs and how beautifully he sang them.

However, Sepperl was not happy just singing. He wanted to play an instrument, too. He had seen the schoolmaster play a violin, and he pretended that he had one too, using two sticks of wood. One stick was the violin, and the other the bow.

When Sepperl was five and a half years old his cousin, Johann Mathias Franck, came to visit the Haydns. Cousin Franck was the schoolmaster and choirmaster of the town of Hainburg. This town was about twelve times larger than Rohrau. When Cousin Franck saw how much talent Sepperl showed, he thought that it would be a good idea to take him to Hainburg. He felt that the boy would have many more opportunities to study if he lived in the larger town. So it was that Sepperl left home at the age of five and a half, to return again only for short visits.

The young boy had much to do in Hainburg. School began at seven in the morning and lasted for six hours, with time off only for lunch. After school there was housework for his cousin's wife, homework and, most important of all, training in music. Joseph was taught the violin and clavier; he sang in the church choir; and the following story is told about how he learned to play the kettle drums the year he was six.

During one of the religious holidays there was to be a procession headed by a drummer. Unfortunately, the drummer died, and there was no one in the village to take his place. "Why not show Joseph the drumstrokes," said Cousin Franck. He is sure to learn quickly." The boy was shown the drumstrokes and left alone to practice. He took a little basket which had been used for baking bread, put a cloth over it, and placed it on a newly upholstered chair. As he drummed away, he did not realize that the flour from the basket was ruining the chair. Joseph was scolded but quickly forgiven when he beat the drums perfectly at the procession. Perhaps, when Haydn wrote his Symphony No. 103 many, many years later, he thought of this incident. The symphony begins with a drumroll, and has been nicknamed *The Drum Roll*. Here is a bar of the music:

Living with Cousin Franck, Joseph did learn a good deal about music, but many times he did not have enough to eat and his clothes were dirty and torn. The Francks were poor, and they had three children of their own to feed and clothe. Somehow none of this mattered to the boy, however, as long as he could study music.

Then the year he was seven, a Mr. George Reuter, the choirmaster at the Cathedral of St. Stephen in Vienna, came to Hainburg to look for new talent. He had heard about young Joseph, and sent for him. Reuter asked the boy to sing a piece of music he had never seen before. The man was amazed at how well the boy did. Next he asked Joseph to sing a trill or *shake* as it was then called.

This is a difficult thing to do because it is two notes sung or played very quickly, one right after the other, and often repeated again and again. Joseph said, "How can you expect me to shake when my cousin does not know how to do it himself?" Reuter showed him how to do it and was so pleased when Joseph did it perfectly that he took a plateful of cherries and emptied it into the boy's pockets. In later years Haydn is supposed to have said that he never could sing a trill without thinking of cherries.

Reuter had to get permission from Joseph's father before they could leave for Vienna, but in a few days the boy and he were off. The Choir School at St. Stephen's Cathedral was Joseph's home for the next nine years.

The surroundings at the choir school were pleasant, but Reuter did not treat the boys well. He did not give them enough to eat. The happiest day for the boys were those when they were invited to sing at the homes of the Viennese nobility; there they were given plenty of good food.

One festival time the choirboys were asked to join the choir at the Royal Court of Maria Theresa. Her castle, called Schönbrunn, had just been built. In fact, the scaffolding was still up around the building, and the boys climbed on top of it with shouts of delight and much laughter. The Empress appeared at the window and, in an angry voice, said, "Anyone who does this once more will receive a good thrashing." The next day Joseph could not resist the temptation, and he did it again. The Empress kept her promise and ordered the capellmeister to give the "fair-haired blockhead the promised punishment."

From that time on things grew worse for Joseph at the choir school. He was getting older, and his voice was changing. His younger brother, Michael, who had just arrived at the school, was able to sing the soprano parts much better than he. Reuter was harsh with Joseph and would not help him with his work. Joseph had to study the rules for composition all by himself, and even when he had completed writing a piece of music, Reuter would not look at it.

Finally things came to a head. During a rehearsal of the choir, Joseph, who was always fond of a practical joke, cut off the pigtail of the boy in front of him. Reuter was furious and said, "You will be caned on the hand." Joseph, now seventeen, thought that much too embarrassing and cried out, "I would rather leave the Cantorei than be caned." Of course Reuter was waiting for this moment, and he said, "You are expelled!"

It was a cold November day when Joseph left St. Stephen's. He had no money and his only possessions were three ragged shirts, a torn coat, and a few books. As he wandered through the lonely streets, wondering what would become of him, he met a gentleman whom he had known, a Mr. Michael Spangler. When the kind man heard of Joseph's plight, he invited the boy to share his own small apartment with him and his wife and his child.

With the help of Mr. Spangler, Joseph was able to find a few piano pupils. He also earned a little money by playing at dances and arranging music for small orchestras. He liked living with the Spanglers, even though the garret was very crowded. Unfortunately, Joseph could not stay because Mrs. Spangler was expecting another baby and there just was not enough room. Joseph had to find another place to live.

Fortunately he met a friend of his father who lent

him enough money to permit him to go on with his studies. Joseph found a place to live and he bought, as he said, "an old worm-eaten clavier" to practice on. He also bought books on composition and music to play. His favorite pieces were the first six sonatas of Philipp Emanuel Bach, the son of Johann Sebastian Bach. Joseph practiced these pieces for hours and hours, and he said that they "opened a new world" for him. It was at this time that Joseph really began to compose.

An Italian poet, named Metastasio, lived a few floors below Joseph. The poet loved music. He listened to Joseph's playing through the open windows and one day, when he met him on the stairs, he introduced himself. He told Joseph that the young daughter of the family with whom he was sharing his apartment, was anxious to study the piano with him. Joseph was delighted, and he gave Marianne daily lessons in exchange for all his meals.

Marianne became an excellent pianist, and she also studied singing with the great Italian teacher, Porpora, who was then living in Vienna. Joseph used to go with Marianne to her lessons and accompany her on the piano. In this way he became friendly with the master. He soon became Porpora's valet just to be near him. For three months he cleaned Porpora's shoes, brushed and arranged his wig, and even listened to the old master call him a blockhead. All this did not matter because young Haydn learned a great deal from Porpora. He learned much about the fundamentals of composition, about singing, and even how to speak Italian.

After three months Haydn returned to his garret and worked harder than ever on his compositions. He originated a new way of writing the first movement of a sonata. What he did is now called *Sonata Form.* There are three sections in Sonata Form, A. B. and A. In section A. the composer writes the themes that he is going to use in the first movement. This is called The Exposition (Statement of Themes). Section B. is the development of these themes, and this is the Development Section. Finally, in section three, which is A. again he repeats the themes that he has used in the first part; this is called the Recapitulation. Here is a bar of the first movement of Haydn's Sonata in D Major:

In the time of Haydn it was important for musicians and composers to know people of the nobility. The Countess Thün was anxious to meet Haydn because she had played some of his sonatas and thought that they were graceful and lovely. When Haydn was brought to her, she could hardly believe her eyes, for he was shy, awkward and badly dressed. However, when she had spent a few minutes with him, she realized how gracious and kind he was. So she immediately arranged to have lessons with him, and it was through her that Haydn met people who were a great help to him.

Haydn was invited to play chamber music at the country home of Karl Joseph von Fürnberg, and it was for this that he composed his first string quartet. This quartet is still popular today. It is known as *The Hunt*.

At one of these chamber music evenings, Haydn met Count Ferdinand Maximillian von Morzin, who engaged Haydn as his musical director. The count and his wife adored music and had two orchestras, one in Vienna in the winter and one in Lukavec, Bohemia, in the summer. Haydn composed his first symphony in Lukavec. Also in Lukavec, Haydn met Prince Paul Esterházy, who was to be his patron for many years.

Just about this time Haydn, now twenty-eight years old, fell in love with one of his pupils, a girl named Therese. However, Therese was very religious, and she entered a convent instead of marrying him. Haydn was very unhappy about this, and Therese's father persuaded him to marry his eldest daughter, Marianna. This was a most unfortunate marriage. Marianna did not like music, and it was said that she used Haydn's manuscripts to line her pastry tins. Sometimes she even used them for hair curlers. Also, Haydn adored children, but Frau Haydn did not. Haydn never had any children of his own.

In a way it was fortunate that one year after Haydn's marriage he was appointed musical director at Esterháza, and he had to leave Vienna. He had so much to do in Esterháza that he forgot his troubles. Haydn composed all the music for the entertainment of Prince Esterházy and his guests. Sometimes it would be an opera for a birthday party. Other times it might be a string quartet or a sonata or even a symphony for a special occasion. He also had to rehearse and conduct all of the concerts. The men in the orchestra loved their "Papa Haydn" as they called him, and they would do anything to please him. If at any time "Papa Haydn" wanted to try something out when he was composing a symphony, he just rang a bell and the men assembled immediately. One day Papa Haydn called them in for what he said was a very important rehearsal. What the men were asked to play was the *Toy Symphony,* which amused them very much. Haydn was the first composer to bring humor into his music.

Haydn has very often been called the "Father of the Symphony. This is not because he invented the symphony, but because he worked out new ideas for it. Haydn added a minuet movement to his symphonies; and his minuets were always played a little faster than minuets had been played before. He often wrote slow introductions for the fast movements of his symphonies and that had not been done before. Haydn used different combinations of instruments for his orchestra, and this changed the sound of the orchestra. He was also the first composer to use mutes on his stringed instruments. A *mute* is a small clamp of brass, ivory, or wood. When this is placed over the bridge of the instrument, it muffles the sound and makes it much softer.

Although Haydn loved his work at Esterháza, he often got tired of it and was happy to have an opportunity to go to Vienna. On one occasion, when he was visiting his friend Mozart, Mozart's father was there. Haydn turned to him and said, "I tell you before God, as an honest man, your son is the greatest composer known to me, either in person or reputation." When Mozart wrote a set of six quartets, which were published in 1785, he dedicated them to his "beloved friend, Haydn." Mozart always said that it was from Haydn that he learned to write quartets.

Haydn's reputation travelled far and wide. King Charles III of Spain requested Haydn to write music on "The Seven Last Words of Our Savior." Haydn wrote the oratorio, and the King was so pleased with it that he sent back a golden snuff box set with diamonds. The King also sent Haydn a large chocolate cake. To

Haydn's surprise, when he cut into the cake, he found it filled with gold pieces!

Later an Englishman named Mr. Salamon came to ask Haydn to come to England to compose new music for some special concerts. These concerts were called The Salamon Concerts. Haydn, who was now sixty years old, was anxious to have a change from Esterháza. He gladly accepted; but when Mozart heard of this he said to Haydn, "Oh, Papa, you have no education for the wide world, and you speak so few languages." Haydn answered, "But my language is understood all over the world."

Haydn made two successful trips to London. Among the works he composed during these visits were the symphonies known as the *London Symphonies*. Sometimes they are called the *Salamon Symphonies*. It was during one of these trips that Haydn was given the degree of Doctor of Music at Oxford University. For this occasion he wrote his Symphony No. 92 in G Major which has always been known as the *Oxford Symphony*.

On Haydn's last trip back from London to Vienna, he stopped in the city of Bonn. Here he met young Beethoven and, after hearing him play, agreed to teach him if he would come to Vienna.

When Haydn finally reached Esterháza, he found that things were not as they had once been. Nicholas, the grandson of Anton, who was now at the head of Esterháza, was not a nice person to work for. He did not pay Haydn very well, and he was very critical of his music. The only kind of music that he wanted Haydn to compose was religious music. At this time Haydn composed six of his Masses, and he also composed his famous oratorio, *The Creation*.

The first performance of *The Creation* was a very exciting one. Although it was given for an invited audience, crowds gathered in the streets just to see Haydn and the nobility arrive. Haydn was so moved by all this that he said, "One moment I was as cold as ice; the next I seemed on fire."

The strain of this excitement and of the conditions at Esterháza, soon began to tell on Haydn's health, and he became quite ill. On May 12, 1809 a great bombardment of Vienna took place and a cannon ball fell near Haydn's home. The house shook, but Haydn said to his servants, "Children, don't be frightened; where Haydn is, nothing can happen to you." Eleven days later Haydn quietly passed away at the age of 77.

Haydn was very much loved and recognized during his lifetime. In his old age he sat in an armchair, always dressed in his finest clothes with his white kid gloves on the table next to him, and received any visitor who might want to see him.

The great master left his personal belongings to his relatives and his faithful servant, Essler, but to the world he left 104 Symphonies, 77 String Quartets, 43 Piano Sonatas many works for other instruments, Masses, Oratorios, Operas and Songs.

Wolfgang Amadeus Mozart

1756–1791

Although Mozart was christened Joannes Chrysotomus Wolfgang Amadeus Mozart, he soon became known just as Wolfgang Amadeus Mozart.

Wolfgang Amadeus Mozart was born on January 27, 1756, in Salzburg, Austria. His father, Leopold, was a violinist in the orchestra of the Archbishop of Salzburg and he was also a teacher of the violin and the clavier. Maria Anna, Wolfgang's sister, was four and a half years old when Wolfgang was born. She had been given the nickname of Nannerl, and she decided to give her little brother a nickname, too. She called him Wolferl.

Wolferl heard music in his home from the time he was a tiny baby. His father gave many lessons at home and one of his best clavier students was Nannerl. The clavier was the instrument that was used before our modern piano.

As soon as Wolferl was able to stand up, he tried to play along with Nannerl. At the age of three, he sat at the clavier and picked out the tunes that he had heard his sister play. To amuse himself further, he played thirds up and down the clavier. *Thirds* are two notes separated by one note in between, as for example C and E. The two notes are struck together, and the sound is a pleasant one.

When Wolferl was only five, he composed his first minuet. This Minuet in F Major is still played. Here are a few bars of the music:

Very often musicians who played in the orchestra with his father came to visit after rehearsals. One day, as Herr Schactner, the court trumpeter, and Mr. Mozart entered the living room, they noticed that Wolferl was sitting at a table writing. When they asked him what he was doing, he said, "I am writing a concerto for the clavier, and when it is finished I will show it to you." In a little while, Wolferl, who was not quite six, brought the "concerto" to his father. There were some inkblots on the paper, but when Wolferl's father examined what the child had written, he could not believe his eyes. "Look, Herr Schactner, how correct and orderly it is. Of course, it could never be of any use, for it is so difficult that no one in the world could play it." Wolferl's answer to this was, "That is why it is a concerto; it must be practiced."

Some years later, when Mozart composed concertos for the piano, he did more to develop the concerto form than any composer had done before him. Up until the time of Mozart, the concerto was nothing more than a harpsichord sonata accompanied by some stringed instruments. In Mozart's concertos, the piano parts blend with the important orchestral parts. Sometimes they even sound like symphonies. Of all the twenty-seven piano concertos that Mozart wrote, there is not one that cannot be called a masterpiece.

At about the same time, when Wolferl was not quite six, a friend of the family gave him a little violin. Although Wolferl begged for lessons, his father felt that his son had enough to do without studying the violin. Then one day a violinist, Wentzl, came to the Mozart home with some trios that he had written. Wentzl played the first violin part, Schactner played the second violin part, and Leopold played the viola. Wolferl begged to play the second violin part along with the men, but his father laughed and said, "You must have lessons first." Wolferl began to cry, and the men let him play along with them. Herr Schactner was so surprised at how well Wolferl played his part that he stopped playing and the boy continued on by himself.

By now Nannerl and Wolferl played the clavier very well together. Leopold was a good teacher, and he worked with the children every day. They were soon referred to as "The Wonder Children of Salzburg."

Leopold was very proud of his children, and he

wanted people in other cities besides Salzburg to hear how wonderful they were.

The first city he planned to take Nannerl and Wolferl to was Munich, the capital of Bavaria. The children had never been on a long coach ride before, and there was much excitement in the Mozart household. The only thing that the children were disappointed about was that Mama, their dog, Frau Bimperl, and their canary, Herr Cannerei, could not go along, too.

When they arrived in Munich, Papa Mozart succeeded in arranging a meeting with the Elector of Bavaria, Maximillian Joseph. He was a good 'cellist himself and he knew much about music. The children played for him, and he was amazed at Nannerl and Wolferl. He was particularly impressed with Wolferl's performance of a concerto. The trip was a success.

In three weeks they returned to Salzburg, but not for long. Leopold borrowed money from his landlord and friend, Lorenz Hagenhouer, and planned a much longer trip. He rented a private coach, and this time Mrs. Mozart went along, too. The children were to play their first concerts in Vienna, the capital of Austria.

On the way to Vienna, the family stopped to rest at a monastery. Wolferl was permitted to play the organ and, as he had never played on such a large one before, he was thrilled with the beautiful sounds that came out of the instrument. The monks were at supper, and when they heard the lovely music, they went into the chapel to see who was playing. They could not believe their eyes when they saw the tiny boy sitting at the organ. However, one of them recognized the children and said, "But that boy is Mozart, one of the wonder children of Salzburg."

After a few days in Vienna, the children were invited to appear at the Royal Palace to play for the Emperor Francis and the Empress Maria Theresa. First the children played together on the clavier, and then Wolferl played solos on the clavier and the violin. When the Emperor put a cloth over the keys and Wolferl played perfectly without even seeing them, the Emperor called the boy a magician. There was much applause and Wolferl was so happy that he ran up to the Empress, put his arms around her, and kissed her. Marie Theresa gave the children beautiful clothes, and Mr. Mozart received 100 ducats, which would be about $225.00 in our money.

Unfortunately, the happy days in Vienna came to a sad end. Wolferl became ill with scarlet fever, and it was weeks before the family could go home.

Back in Salzburg once more, the children worked harder than ever. Their father was secretly planning another trip, and he wanted his children to be the sensation of Europe.

The Mozarts left Salzburg on June 9, 1763 and did not return until November 30, 1766.

Mr. Mozart was what we would call a good press agent. In advance of the children's performances, he would write articles for the papers, telling about the many accomplishments of his "wonder children." People were curious and came to the concerts. The famous German author, Goethe, then 14, was in the audience at one of the first concerts of the trip in Frankfurt, and he became one of Wolfgang's great admirers.

After Frankfurt, Paris was the next big stop. But on the way the children gave concerts in Coblentz and Brussels. They received so many gifts that their father said, "With snuff boxes and such we shall soon be able to fit out a shop."

Paris was friendly and gay. On Christmas Eve, 1763, the King, Louis XV, invited the Mozarts to the famous palace of Versailles. The family remained in the palace for two weeks, and the children gave several successful concerts. It was at this time that Wolferl composed four sonatas for violin and piano, and his father had them published. In a letter to a friend, Mr. Mozart wrote, "Picture to yourself the furor they will make in the world when people read on the title page that they have been composed by a seven year old child."

These sonatas are still played; they are listed as K. 6, K. 7, K. 8, and K. 9. The K. stands for Ludwig van Köchel, who was an Austrian musician. In 1862 he made a listing of Mozart's works according to the dates when they were composed. The last work of Mozart was *The Requiem,* K. 626.

After five months in Paris, the family went to London. There Wolfgang heard Handel's music for the first time, and he particularly loved the horn parts. His first symphony was written here as a surprise for his father who had been ill. While he was composing it, he turned to his sister and said, "Remind me to give something really good to the horns."

When they returned to Salzburg, Wolfgang was ten years old and he had already become known as a composer. In order to impress the Archbishop, he composed an oratorio especially for him.

The stay in Salzburg was a short one however, for the family soon went to Vienna again. Unfortunately there was an epidemic of smallpox in Vienna, and the children became seriously ill. It was a miracle that their lives were saved. While Wolfgang was recovering, he wrote his first two operas: *La Finta Semplice* and *Bastien und Bastienne*. These operas are still performed.

At that time Mr. Mozart decided that he must take Wolfgang to Italy. He felt that only in Italy could the young composer learn to write operas. So Nannerl and Mrs. Mozart went home to Salzburg, and Wolfgang and his father left for Italy.

During the Italian trip Wolfgang wrote many letters to his mother and sister. He always included little nonsense bits for Frau Bimperl and Herr Cannerei.

In Milan, Wolfgang wrote the opera *Mithridates, King of Pontius*. He conducted the first performance of this opera himself, and people shouted, "Bravo, long live the Master."

In Rome, Wolfgang and his father went to the Sistine Chapel to hear a performance of the *Miserere*. This music was considered so sacred that it was not permitted out of the Vatican.

Wolfgang listened to it very carefully, and when he and his father went back to their rooms, he wrote it out note for note. The Pope heard about this, sent for Wolfgang, and conferred upon him the "Order of the Golden Spur."

When Wolfgang and his father returned to Salzburg after the exciting Italian trip, life seemed rather dull there. Wolfgang was twenty-one, and he felt old enough to go to Paris by himself. But his father insisted that his mother go with him. The two arrived in Paris on March 23, 1778.

Somehow things in Paris were not as Wolfgang had expected them to be. Some people remembered him as the "wonder child" of seven, but most were slow to accept him as the mature musician of twenty-one. He did have a few pupils, and he was asked to write some ballet music, but that was not what he had hoped for. He wanted someone to commission him to write a great opera. Since no one carried out Mozart's desire, he tried to forget his disappointment by composing other kinds of music. Among his works at this time were the Symphony Number 31, known as the *Paris Symphony,* some sonatas for violin and piano, and some piano sonatas. The most popular piano sonata of this group is the Sonata in A Major, known as the *Alla Turca.* It is the third movement of the sonata, the rondo, that has given it its nickname.

Here are a few measures of the *Rondo alla Turca:*

The Paris trip came to a sad end when Wolfgang's mother died quite suddenly. Wolfgang wrote home to tell his father the unhappy news, and his father begged him to return to Salzburg as soon as possible.

Wolfgang stopped in Munich to see Aloysia Weber, a charming girl with whom he had fallen in love. He thought that seeing her would make him a little happier. Poor Wolfgang! She did not love him anymore, and she was going to marry someone else.

Wolfgang went home to Salzburg. His next two and a half years were spent there, but they were unhappy ones. He worked for the Archbishop and disliked it. Finally he decided to leave Salzburg and go to live in Vienna.

When Mozart arrived in Vienna, he found that the

Webers were living there. Since they had rooms for rent, he moved in with them. He also found that Aloysia's sister, Constanza, now 18, had become a sweet and charming young lady. He fell in love with her, and they decided to get married. However, when Wolfgang wrote to his father for approval, Mr. Mozart did not feel that Constanza would make a suitable wife for him. But Wolfgang had made up his mind. On August 4, 1782 he and Constanza were married. Mr. Mozart finally accepted the marriage, but the relationship between father and son was never again very friendly.

The marriage was a good one, but life in Vienna was not easy for the Mozarts. Somehow, Mozart was never able to find a patron, and in those days it was difficult to manage without one. Wolfgang had some pupils and he gave concerts, but that was hardly enough. Constanza was ill much of the time, and the debts piled up.

In spite of all these difficulties, Mozart composed one masterpiece after another. The music just seemed to flow from him like a river. It was at this time that Haydn and he became good friends. These two great composers did more to develop the writing of string quartets than any composers had ever done before.

Mozart also became friendly with the Italian poet, Lorenzo da Ponte. Da Ponte wrote the librettos for three of Mozart's most famous operas, *The Marriage of Figaro, Don Giovanni* and *Cossi fan Tutte* or *The School for Lovers.*

There is an amusing story about the opera *Don Giovanni,* which was first given in Prague in October, 1787. The night before the opera was to have its opening performance, Mozart still had not written the overture for it. Constanza and he were up all that night. Wolfgang composed the overture, and Constanza read fairy stories to him in order to keep him awake. At seven in the morning the parts were hurried to the copyist, and they were still a little damp when the performance was given that night. No one in the audience knew that the orchestra was playing the difficult music at first sight. The performance was a great success! In this opera Mozart originated what is known as romantic opera.

The next years were filled with sickness and many worries. Mozart received news of his father's death, and that made him very unhappy. Constanza was expecting another baby, and she was not well. She had to go to Baden to take special baths. Although Mozart had been composing one great work after another, the musicians in Vienna did not give him the recognition he deserved. This upset him more than anything else.

It was at this time, when Mozart was lonely and miserable, that a friend came to him with an idea for a new opera. The opera was to be about magic. The story was called *The Magic Flute.* Mozart was fascinated with the libretto, and he started to work on the music immediately. Somehow, working on *The Magic Flute* seemed to bring Mozart a change of luck. Constanza had another son, and her health was much better; and Mozart was asked to compose two other works, a requiem and another opera.

The requiem, which is a Mass for the dead, had a mystery attached to it. One day a stranger appeared and handed Mozart a letter. The letter was unsigned, and it requested Mozart to compose a requiem as soon as possible. He was offered 100 Ducats for his work and was told not to try to find out who wrote the letter. This was all very puzzling, but Mozart agreed to do it because he needed the money.

The other work was to be a new opera in honor of the coronation of Emperor Leopold II, in Prague. The opera was to be ready by the beginning of September, and it was already mid-August. Mozart put both *The Magic Flute* and the requiem away and, together with Constanza and one of his most talented pupils, Herr Süssmayer, left for Prague.

Mozart wrote the music of the opera, *La Clemenza di Tito,* at breakneck speed; his pupil helped him fill in the parts for the orchestra. The performance of the opera was not a success, and Mozart became ill. The strain had been too much for him.

They returned to Vienna and Mozart, still ailing, finished the *Magic Flute* exactly two days before it was to be performed. This opera, with its mystery, humor and real comedy was a great success. Mozart was the first composer to have written a great fairy opera!

The mysterious stranger appeared once more and requested the requiem. Mozart had still not finished it. Although he was quite ill and confined to his bed, he set to work on it in great haste. At one point he looked at Constanza and said, "It is for myself I am writing the requiem."

Suddenly Mozart took a turn for the worse, and he asked that four of his musician friends come to his bed and sing parts of the requiem for him. He began to weep because he realized that he would never finish this work. Mozart died that very night, December 5, 1791, and his pupil Süssmayer finished the requiem.

The mystery of the requiem was solved after Mozart's death. It was discovered that a wealthy amateur musician, Count Walsegg, wanted the requiem written in honor of his wife who had died recently. He wanted people to think that he himself had written the music.

The funeral of the great Mozart was a lonely one. There were only a few friends present, and Constanza was so ill that she had to remain at home. No one has ever been able to find where Mozart was buried because his grave was an unmarked one.

The amount of remarkable music that Mozart composed in his short lifetime of thirty-five years has always seemed a miracle.

Among his works are 41 Symphonies, 27 Piano Concertos, 19 Piano Sonatas, Sonatas for Violin and Piano, Chamber Music, other Orchestral Works, 20 Operas, and many art songs, or *lieder* as they are called. Mozart was one of the first composers to write lieder. He paved the way for Schubert, Schumann, and Brahms. The genius of this great composer will never be forgotten.

Ludwig van Beethoven

1770—1827

The actual date of Ludwig van Beethoven's birth has never been a definite one. It is thought that he was born on December 16, 1770, in Bonn, Germany. However, the only clue is the day on which he was baptized, December 17. It was the custom in those days to baptize babies the day after they were born, so December 16 has been accepted as Beethoven's birthday.

Ludwig's father, Johann, was a singer in the Court of the Elector of Bonn. Ludwig's grandfather, Louis, who died when the boy was only three years old, was also a musician in the court orchestra.

Johann was quick to recognize Ludwig's talent for music. He gave the boy his first lessons on the piano and the violin when he was just four years old. No doubt Johann had dreams of making another Mozart out of his son. Unfortunately, he was not as patient and understanding as Mozart's father had been. During these first lessons there were many tears shed. The boy did not like to practice scales and exercises; he preferred to sit at the piano and make up his own pieces. His father would have none of this, and when he heard Ludwig composing he would rush into the room, spank him, and shout, "What stupid stuff are you scraping at now? You know I can't stand hearing it; play the notes in front of you or all your scraping will amount to nothing."

Ludwig was also sent to the public schools where he learned reading, writing, and a little Latin. He had no friends at school because he was shy and preferred to spend his time dreaming about music.

When Ludwig was nine years old, his father decided he had nothing more to teach his son. The boy must have another teacher. The old court organist, Van den Eeden, accepted Ludwig as his pupil. He taught the boy organ as well as piano. Ludwig learned how to play the organ so quickly that a short time after he started lessons the organist in the Franciscan monastery in Bonn permitted him to play an entire service by himself.

About this time a musician named Tobias Friedrich Pfeiffer came to live with the Beethovens. In exchange for his room, he gave Ludwig piano lessons. It was said that many times, late at night, Pfeiffer and Ludwig's father would return home after drinking too much wine, would awaken Ludwig, and would keep him at the piano until morning.

When Ludwig was ten years old, things were not going well for Johann and the family was quite poor. So Ludwig's mother decided to take her son on a concert tour in Holland. He played in the homes of some of the wealthy families, and everyone was astonished at his ability. The boy was given valuable presents and also some money for his performances.

The following year Ludwig began to study with the newly appointed court organist, Christian Gottlob Neefe. He was an excellent musician and a great help to young Beethoven. Ludwig learned to play all the forty-eight Preludes and Fugues of Johann Sebastian Bach. This is still considered a great accomplishment and especially so when the pianist is only eleven. Herr Neefe also encouraged Ludwig to go ahead with his own compositions. When the young composer wrote *Nine Variations on a March by Dressler,* Neefe had them published for him. These variations are very lovely, and they are still played. Beethoven's first three piano sonatas were written at this time, and they were published two years later, when he was only thirteen. Here are a few measures of the one in E♭ major:

When Neefe occasionally was called away from Bonn, he left young Beethoven in charge of conducting the musical services. This was a great honor for a boy of eleven and a half. Ludwig was given his first payed position when he was thirteen years old. Max Franz, the newly appointed Elector of Bonn, made him the second Court Organist.

There is not much information about Beethoven's life from the years 1784 to 1787. But it is known that in the late spring of 1787, when Beethoven was seventeen, an old dream came true. A friend of his in Bonn made it possible for him to go on a trip to Vienna. This city was then the center of musical life in Germany. Soon after Beethoven arrived in Vienna, he went to play for Mozart. After he had played a few pieces, Mozart gave him a theme to improvise on. To improvise means to compose and play music on the spur of the moment. Ludwig did this so beautifully that Mozart said, "Pay attention to him; he will make a noise in the world some day or other."

Unfortunately, Ludwig was not able to stay in Vienna for more than two months because news came that his mother was dying. Back in Bonn, after an anxious and wearisome journey, Ludwig found his mother frail and motionless on her bed. A few days later, on July 17, 1787, she passed away.

After that, things went from bad to worse. Ludwig's father grew more shiftless after the death of his wife, and many times he would spend all his money on liquor. Ludwig had to become head of the household and take care of his two younger brothers, aged thirteen and eleven. As Ludwig had no money, he appealed to the Elector for help. It was arranged that half of Mr. Beethoven's salary would be given to Ludwig before his father had a chance to spend it.

To help his family still more, Ludwig began to teach the piano. He became acquainted with a family called Breuning and taught two of the children. Frau Breuning was a fine woman; she was like a mother to Ludwig. He stayed at the Breuning home for days at a time. It was there that Ludwig met some very cultured people from whom he learned a great deal about literature. He began to read Shakespeare, and for the first time he read

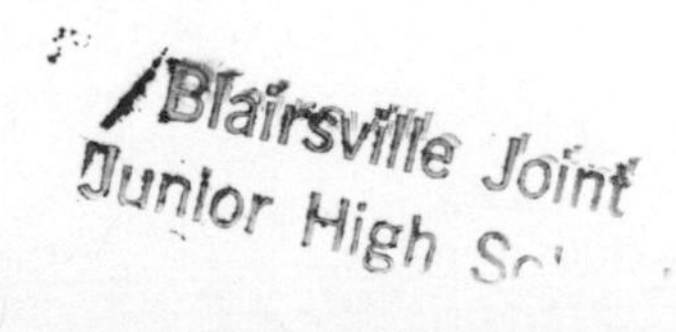

some poems of the great German author, Goethe.

One of the people Ludwig met at the Breunings was Count Ferdinand Ernst Gabriel Waldstein. The two became good friends. Count Waldstein was an amateur musician. He once gave Beethoven a theme upon which the composer wrote piano variations for four hands. These *Variations on A Theme of Count Waldstein* are still played. The Count helped Beethoven in all sorts of ways. Beethoven was very proud; he did not like to accept money from his friends. Count Waldstein gave him money in such a way that it appeared to be a gift from the Elector. It was with Count Waldstein's help that Beethoven was appointed violist of the Opera Orchestra at Bonn. Count Waldstein even sent Beethoven a new piano in place of his old broken one. Beethoven never forgot his friend. Many years later, when he wrote his Piano Sonata in C Major, Opus 53, he dedicated it to Count Waldstein. It has always been known as *The Waldstein Sonata.*

When Beethoven was twenty years old, Haydn passed through Bonn on his way back from London. Beethoven met him and gave the old master a cantata. Haydn was so impressed with the work that he offered to teach Beethoven if he would come to Vienna. With the financial help of the Elector of Bonn, Beethoven left for Vienna. He never returned to Bonn again.

Beethoven's lessons with Haydn were not very successful. Papa Haydn could not understand the impatient young Beethoven, who did not like to follow strict rules. Although he never quarreled with Haydn, Beethoven was known to have said, "Though I had some instruction from Haydn, I never learned anything from him." However, Beethoven admired Haydn's music very much, and Beethoven's early music was influenced by the music of Papa Haydn.

Albrechtsberger, who was Beethoven's next teacher, was also displeased with the young composer who wanted to do things in his own way. He was supposed to have remarked to another pupil, "Oh, that Beethoven, he has learnt nothing, and he will never do anything in decent style." Beethoven's ideas were too revolutionary for these old masters.

However, Beethoven's beautiful piano playing and his great talent for improvisation made him many friends in Vienna. His best friends at this time were the Prince and Princess Lichnowsky. The Prince played both the piano and the violin, and there was always much music in the palace. Beethoven met the fat, jolly violinist, Schuppanzigh, at the Lichnowsky's. Schuppanzigh had his own string quartet and every Friday morning the quartet played in the palace. They would play Beethoven's quartets as soon as he composed them.

The Prince and Princess Lichnowsky wanted Beethoven to come and live in the palace, but he would not do this. Beethoven did not like "royal ways," as he put it; and once in a fit of anger, he is supposed to have said to his friend, Prince Lichnowsky, "You are only a prince. I am Beethoven." The Prince was a kind man, and he forgave Beethoven. He even arranged to give the composer a sum of money annually.

Many stories are told about Beethoven's absentmindedness. Sometimes when Beethoven was having dinner at his favorite tavern, he would become so excited when a theme came into his head that he would forget to order dinner. Then he would scold the waitress for not giving him a bill!

Beethoven always carried a sketchbook with him, and he was constantly writing down his musical ideas.

Sometimes he would have several ideas for the same composition. He would work on his pieces for months and even years before he was satisfied. Fortunately, all of the sketchbooks have been preserved. The originals are now in the British Museum in London, in Leipzig, Germany, and in Vienna, Austria. But copies have been made, and they can be found in any big library.

In Beethoven's early Vienna days he tried to dress in the fashion of the times. He wore silk stockings, a wig, long boots, and a sword, and he carried a double eyeglass and a seal ring. But he soon tired of all this fuss and became quite untidy in his appearance. His clothes always looked torn and ragged. Some of his friends were annoyed at his carelessness and often played a practical joke on him. At night they would creep into his bedroom, take out his old clothes, and substitute a new outfit. Beethoven would dress in the morning and never even notice the difference.

Beethoven was fond of playing jokes on people himself. Sometimes it was just horseplay, and he would roar with laughter when he talked about it. He often acted impulsively. When he got angry, he threw books, plates, and eggs at his servants; when a waiter served stew improperly, he poured the stew over the waiter's head; when a lady wrote and asked him for a lock of his hair, he sent her a wisp of a goat's beard.

At the age of twenty-eight, Beethoven suddenly began to have violent noises in his ears. This proved to be the beginning of incurable deafness.

At first Beethoven went from doctor to doctor, hoping that someone might have a cure for him. One doctor, in whom he had a great deal of faith, a Dr. Schmidt, suggested that he go to a quiet place in the country for a rest cure. Beethoven was happy to take this advice because, as he said, "No man loves the country more than I do." He went to the beautiful Heilingstadt which means *Holy City*. He wandered through the tranquil woods and meadows with his sketchbook as his companion. But even here there were things to depress him. When he saw a shepherd playing a flute, he could hardly hear the sounds that came out. His hearing was getting worse instead of better. It was discouraging, but he was able to overcome his disappointment and work harder than ever on his compositions.

After the summer of 1808, Beethoven returned to Vienna. He had finished his Fifth Symphony, the one known as the *Fate Symphony,* and the Sixth, the *Pastoral Symphony*.

At this time the Archduke Rudolph became Beethoven's friend and pupil. The Archduke, together with Prince Kinsky and Prince Lobkowitz, gave Beethoven an income so that he would not have to worry about money. Beethoven dedicated many of his compositions to his royal friends.

By 1815 Beethoven had completed eight of his nine symphonies, his five piano concertos, his only opera, *Fidelio,* and much chamber music.

It was in the year 1815 that Beethoven had still another misfortune. His brother, Karl, died and Beethoven became the guardian of his nephew, who was also called Karl. This brought nothing but unhappiness to Beethoven. He loved his nephew very much and tried to do everything for him, but the boy was impossible. He ran away from home several times; he stole money; and he was arrested and even tried to kill himself.

From 1816 to 1818 Beethoven was so disturbed that he composed very little. But once again he showed that he could conquer all! In 1818 he began his great Ninth

Symphony or *Choral Symphony* as it is sometimes called. For the first time in the history of music, words were introduced into a symphony. At the end of the symphony Beethoven wrote music for a chorus and solo singers for the words of Schiller's *Ode To Joy*. Here are a few bars of this magnificent music.

The symphony was not performed until May 7, 1824. Beethoven conducted the first performance. He was completely deaf by this time and, at the end of the symphony, when the applause was like thunder, he kept right on facing the musicians. Someone had to turn him around so that he could see the applauding audience.

Beethoven had done many new things in his compositions. In the piano sonata, the *Pathetique,* he had used a slow introduction, an adagio, as it is called, at the beginning of the first movement. In the *Moonlight Sonata,* Beethoven wrote the first movement in a free way, not at all in the Sonata Form that first movements were usually written in. Whenever rules interfered with the beautiful sounds that Beethoven wanted to have, he changed the rules.

In the last years of his life, he continued to be worried by his nephew. It is believed that Beethoven died sooner than he might have because of the carelessness of his nephew. Beethoven had taken Karl to the country because the boy had been ill; and when they were returning to Vienna in an open coach, Beethoven caught a very bad cold. Karl did not call a doctor as soon as he should have, and Beethoven became steadily worse. Pneumonia set in. Beethoven died on March 26,

1827, during a terrific thunderstorm. It seemed that even the heavens were angry!

Beethoven was buried in the Währing Cemetery in Vienna. On the day of the funeral all the schools were closed. Twenty thousand people crowded the square to see the funeral procession. A stranger, seeing the enormous crowds, asked an old woman what was happening, and she said, "Do you not know they are burying the general of the musicians?"

The great Beethoven left much marvelous music. Among his masterpieces are nine symphonies, 32 piano sonatas, violin sonatas, 'cello sonatas, much chamber music, songs and one opera, *Fidelio.* There are also many smaller pieces like *Für Elise, The Rage Over The Lost Penny,* and *With Two Eyeglasses Obligato.*

Besides his music, Beethoven left some letters addressed to an "Immortal Beloved." Beethoven was in love many times, but no one has been able to discover who the "Immortal Beloved" really was.

Every year, people from all over the world now visit the *Beethovenhaus,* the house in Bonn where Beethoven was born. The rooms are filled with relics and pictures from every part of his life. Beethoven's manuscripts are kept in glass cases, and his piano stands in the same place it always stood. Even his ear trumpets are kept on a little table near his bed.

Franz Peter Schubert

1797—1828

Franz Peter Schubert, the greatest of all the composers of songs, or *Lieder* as they are called in German, was born in Vienna, Austria, on January 31, 1797. The city of Vienna had long been a center of musical life, and many composers lived there at one time or another. But Franz Schubert, or Franzl, as he was called when he was a boy, was the first famous composer to be born there.

Franzl's father was a schoolmaster, and his family was a large one. Schoolmasters did not earn very much, and Frau Schubert had a hard time managing the household. However, the family was a happy one, and there was always much singing and playing in the home.

Several of the fourteen children showed musical talent, but Franzl was the most gifted of them all. When he was only four, he picked out his first tunes on the piano. When he was six, he had violin lessons with his father and piano lessons with his big brother, Ignaz. It did not take long for Franzl to learn all that his father and Ignaz had to teach him, and another teacher had to be found. Michael Holzer, the parish choirmaster, was his next teacher. He taught Franzl piano, violin, organ, singing, and the theory of music. Holzer was so astonished at the boy's progress that he said to Mr. Schubert, "Whenever I want to teach him anything new, he already knows it. I never had such a pupil before." When Franzl was not quite eleven, he became the first soprano in the Lichtenthal choir; and whenever violin solos were required for the service, he was able to play them, too.

Mr. Schubert soon realized how gifted his son was and decided that Franzl must try to get into The Imperial Convict. This was a fine school, in spite of its strange name, and it was there that musicians were trained for the court chapel.

The day arrived for Franzl's audition. He got all dressed up in a grey suit that his mother had made for him. Unfortunately, the suit did not fit him very well, and the funny hat he wore did not help. The other boys, who were also waiting to be heard, took one look at him, giggled, and even cracked jokes about him. They called him The Miller. The boys must have been embarrassed when Franzl sang so beautifully that he was the only one to be accepted. His "miller's suit" was changed for the gold-laced uniform of the Imperial Choristers.

Franzl was very busy at school. He played the violin in the orchestra, sang in the choir, and also studied mathematics, history, geography, writing, drawings, and languages. The orchestra rehearsed every day, and Franzl's favorite symphony was the one in G minor by Mozart. Whenever the boys played this symphony, Franzl said, "You can hear the angels singing in this music."

Sitting in front of Franzl in the orchestra was an older boy named Michael Spaun. One day Michael turned around to see who was playing the violin so beautifully. He was surprised to see that the fine violinist was a small boy with big spectacles. Franzl always had to wear thick glasses because he was very near-sighted. The two boys became great friends. Franzl confided in Michael, telling about his compositions and about a piano piece he had just written called a *Fantasie,* which was thirty-two pages long. Franzl also told his friend that there were many more compositions in his head but he did not have enough money to buy music paper. After this Michael saw to it that Franzl always had enough music paper.

When Sundays and holidays came, Franz was particularly happy because he was permitted to go home. There was always much music when Franz came home. If he had composed a new quartet, his father would play the 'cello part, Ferdinand and Ignaz, his two older brothers, would play the first and second violin parts, and Franz would play the viola part. His father would make a mistake now and then and Franz would say, with a smile, "Herr Vater, something must be wrong there."

Franz stayed at The Convict until he was seventeen. During this time he composed much music, including his first symphony. His instrumental music was very song-like and beautiful, but it was in songs themselves that Franz showed his greatest talent.

Once out of school, Franz had to decide whether he would go into the army or go to a Normal School and become a teacher. He went to the Normal School at St. Anna; and when his studies were finished, he became his father's assistant at the school.

Teaching little children, Franz soon discovered, was not what he really enjoyed. He was happiest when his work was over and he could write down the lovely tunes that had come into his head during the day. He was also happy when he could spend the evenings with his new friends, the Grob family. They were a fine family, and they loved music. Therese, the daughter, had a good voice and enjoyed the songs Franz brought her. He had just composed a Mass, and Therese sang the solo part at the first public performance. Salieri, the court capellmeister, was in the audience. He was so impressed with the Mass that he offered to teach Franz. After one year of study, Franz had composed, among other works, 146 songs. One of these was the well-known *Erlking*.

The words for the *Erlking* are a poem by the German poet, Goethe. In it he describes a father riding on a black horse, through the dark forest at midnight, in search of a doctor for his sick child, whom he holds clasped in his arms. Schubert's music is dramatic and, in the following bars of the piano introduction, you can hear the galloping of the horse!

Franz had two more wonderful friends. One of them was the poet Johann Mayrhofer, who wrote many verses that Franz set to music. The other was a young man named Franz von Schober. He was so enthusiastic about Schubert's songs that he invited him to come and live with him so that he would not have to teach anymore. Schubert happily accepted, delighted that he could now devote all of his time to music.

One day von Schober brought an important singer named Vogl to the room. The two men found Franz hard at work. Music sheets covered the floor as well as the table and chairs. Vogl picked up song after song and hummed it through. He was much impressed and called the songs "divine inspirations." Vogl and Schubert became great friends, and the singer performed many of Schubert's works.

On one occasion Schubert gave Vogl some manuscripts to take home. Among them was a song that the singer particularly liked, but it was written in a key that was too low; so Vogl had it copied out in a higher key. About two weeks later, when Schubert and he were going over this song, Schubert exclaimed in a loud voice, "I say, this song's not so bad; whose is it?" Schubert wrote so many songs, and he wrote them so quickly, that he could not even remember this one.

One Sunday afternoon Schubert was out for a stroll with some of his friends. As they passed a beer garden, they saw another friend sitting at a small table and they stopped to chat with him. Schubert noticed a volume of Shakespeare on the table and picked it up to glance through it. The poem "Hark! Hark! the Lark" caught his eye and he began to read it. Suddenly he exclaimed, "Such a lovely melody has come into my head! If only I had some music paper." Someone drew a staff on back of a menu, and there in the middle of all the noise Schubert wrote his beautiful song *Hark, hark the Lark.*

In the summer of 1818 Schubert had to move from the room he shared with von Schober. Von Schober's brother was coming to live there, and the room was not big enough for three. Fortunately, Schubert had just been offered the position of music teacher in the family of Count Johann Esterházy. Even though he did not enjoy teaching, Schubert accepted the offer and went to the country estate of the Esterházy's at Zselesy, Hungary. He did not mind the change as much as he thought he would. He did miss Vienna and his friends, but the Esterházy family was a musical one and Schubert enjoyed teaching their two daughters. In fact, it was said that he fell in love with one of them, but he knew that he would never be accepted in a class of society not his own.

It was during Schubert's stay at the Esterházy's that he heard many gypsy and Hungarian melodies. They were played and sung by the people in the village and by the servants in the house. He loved these tunes and used them in his dances, in his marches, and even in his chamber music. Schubert also composed a great many four-hand pieces for the piano during this Hungarian Period. He probably composed some of them for the Esterházy daughters because they enjoyed playing duets. Among these compositions is a set of three military marches. The most popular one of the set is the March in D Major, known as *Marche Militaire.* Although it was originally written for four hands, it has been arranged in many different ways.

Here are a few bars of the arrangement for solo piano:

As time went by, Schubert began to write more and more music for four hands. Next to his songs, it is in this kind of composition that he did his most important work. It can be said that he created the form of four-hand music.

At one time Schubert wrote a set of variations on a French tune for four hands, which he especially dedicated to Beethoven. He had never met Beethoven and wanted to take the composition to him personally. He was too shy to go alone, so he asked the publisher, Diabelli, to come along to introduce him. Beethoven was pleased to meet Schubert and extremely happy about having the variations dedicated to him. As he glanced through the music, he noticed a bar of music that he did not quite understand. Being completely deaf at the time, he handed a piece of paper and a pencil to Schubert so that he could explain it. Schubert was so overcome with shyness that he ran from the house and never met Beethoven again.

Until the time Schubert was almost twenty-five, not one of his many compositions had been published. Publishers did not think his music was the kind people would buy. Finally some of Schubert's friends had the song *The Erlking* printed, and one hundred copies were sold immediately. The money received was given to the publishers Cappi and Diabelli to cover the costs of publishing several other of Schubert's songs.

These songs were very successful, and then the publishers realized what a mistake they had made. After this, they bought many of Schubert's manuscripts from him but, unfortunately, Schubert sold them for practically nothing.

Schubert had no sense of the value of money. As soon as he received some, he would call his friends together for a celebration. They would meet at the Gasthous, which was like one of our modern clubs, and would have a merry time until most of Schubert's money was gone. For days after that Schubert would have money enough only to buy biscuits and coffee for dinner.

Schubert worked hour after hour composing new music. It was said that sometimes he went to bed with his spectacles on, to save the time of putting them on in the morning.

Besides 603 songs, operas, many piano compositions, pieces for other instruments, chamber music, and church music, Schubert wrote ten symphonies. The most popular one of the symphonies is *The Unfinished.* No one knows why Schubert did not finish this symphony. It was not his last one. The last symphony is the one in C Major, called *The Great.* This final symphony was discovered quite by accident. When the composer Robert Schumann moved to Vienna, he went to visit Schubert's favorite brother, Ferdinand. Franz had been living with his brother for some time before he died. As Schumann looked around the room, he noticed a pile of manuscripts on the table; and it was among these that he found the symphony called *The Great,* which he nicknamed *The Symphony of Heavenly Lengths.* It is Schubert's longest symphony, and it takes one hour to play.

In other pieces Schubert did something few other composers have done, he repeated himself. For example, he loved his song *The Wanderer* so much that he quoted himself by using a few bars of it in his piano piece called *The Wanderer*. Almost the same thing happened in his quintet *The Trout*. This time a good friend of Schubert, who was especially fond of the composer's song *The Trout* asked him to use a few measures of it in another composition. He did. This time he wrote six variations on the theme of his song and used them in a quintet called *The Trout*. This is a piece played by a piano, violin, viola, 'cello, and double bass.

About the end of October, 1828, Schubert became seriously ill. For many days he could not eat at all and no medicine seemed to help. He became weaker and weaker, and finally on November 19, 1828, he died.

Many of Schubert's faithful friends came to his funeral, and he was buried in the Währing Cemetery very close to Beethoven. This had been his final request.

In Vienna, many memorials have been set up for Schubert. Among them are a special tablet on the house where he was born and one on the house where he died. There is also a large seated marble figure of Schubert in the *Stadt Park* (City Park).

Felix Mendelssohn

1809—1847

Jakob Ludwig Felix Mendelssohn-Bartholdy, known today as Felix Mendelssohn, was born in Hamburg, Germany, on February 3, 1809. His father, Abraham, was a banker, and his grandfather, Moses, was a philosopher. When Felix had become an important composer, his father jokingly said, "Formerly, I was the son of my father, now I am the father of my son."

The Mendelssohns were a happy and prosperous family. Felix had none of the money worries of Mozart, Beethoven, or Schubert. The only disturbing thing in his childhood happened when Felix was just three. Then French soldiers occupied Hamburg and life for the German families was very unpleasant. The Mendelssohn family disguised themselves and fled to Berlin. In Berlin, Felix's grandmother had a beautiful large house on an avenue called the *Neue Promenade,* and the family moved in with her.

There were three other children in the family besides Felix: Fanny, Rebecka, and Paul. Fanny was the oldest, and Felix adored her. The two children were always together.

Felix's mother, Leah, was a very cultured woman; she knew a great deal about art, literature, and music. The children loved to have their mother play the piano and sing songs, but they liked best of all the times when she read stories and poems to them.

It is not known how well Leah played the piano, but it is known that she taught Felix and Fanny to play when they were quite small. At first she thought that Fanny was the more talented of the two, and she would say, "Fanny has got Bach fugue fingers." Everyone knew how difficult it was to play Bach fugues! Even after the children were studying with other teachers, their mother sat close by, with her knitting in her hands, and listened to them practice.

Fanny and Felix progressed rapidly; and when the family went on a trip to Paris, the children studied with a fine teacher called Mme. Bigot. She thought Fanny and Felix were most remarkable and was sorry when they had to go home.

When the family returned to Berlin, Fanny and Felix really began to study hard. They had to get up at five o'clock in the morning every day except Sunday in order to get all their work done. They studied the piano, violin, composition, Greek, Latin, drawing, and many other school subjects. Carl Zelter, who taught them musical composition, was the most helpful of all their teachers.

In spite of the great amount of work the children

had to do, they still had wonderful times together. They were both just beginning to compose, and Felix would improvise amusing music about anything unusual that happened during the day. The two children shrieked with laughter at the funny music and words that Felix made up.

When Felix was nine years old, he appeared in public for the first time. He played the piano part of a trio for piano and two horns that was written by a composer of the times called Woelfl.

When Felix was eleven, he entered the singing class of the Singakademie. A few months later he composed a cantata.

By the time Felix was twelve years old, he had composed fifty or sixty works. He did his work in a very systematic way. On the manuscript of each of his pieces he wrote the date and place of composition. He kept this habit up throughout his whole life. Most of his manuscripts have been preserved and are in the State Library at Berlin.

There were always musical evenings in the Mendelssohn home; and now that Felix was composing so much music, special concerts were given every other Sunday so that the young composer's works could be heard. A small orchestra was formed, with Felix as the conductor, and the concerts were held in the large dining room of the house.

At the time of these concerts Felix was a little more than twelve years old, and he was still quite short. In order that the men in the orchestra could see him, Felix had to stand on a stool.

There was always an audience at these concerts; if any musician of note were passing through Berlin, he was invited. Zelter, Felix's composition teacher, was always present. His criticisms of Felix's compositions were most valuable.

Zelter was a good friend of the great German poet, Goethe, and, at about this time, Zelter was invited to visit the poet in Weimar. Zelter was very enthusiastic about his gifted pupil, Felix, and decided to take him along so that the aging Goethe would have an opportunity to meet the boy and hear him play. Everyone in the Mendelssohn home thought that this was a wonderful idea. Fanny was the most excited one of all.

When Felix and his teacher arrived at Goethe's home, Felix found the following letter from his sister Fanny:

"When you are with Goethe, I advise you to open your eyes and ears wide, and after you come home, if you can't repeat every word that fell from his mouth, I will have nothing more to do with you."

Felix was thrilled to be with the great old man, and Goethe was very much impressed with Felix. The visit lasted for two weeks, and during that time Felix played many of his compositions for Goethe. He also played Bach fugues, and he was able to read at sight any music that Goethe put in front of him. Once when Goethe had invited some guests, Felix amazed everyone with an improvisation upon a theme that Zelter gave him. Zelter himself was so surprised that he said, "What goblins and dragons have you been dreaming about to drive you along so wildly." Felix and Goethe became good friends, and Felix made several more trips to visit Goethe.

Felix spent the next few years working very hard on his compositions. He wrote symphonies, quartets, piano pieces, songs, and short operas. One of these operas was called *Der Onkel aus Boston* (*The Uncle from Boston*). This work was performed at the Sunday morning concert on Felix's fifteenth birthday.

After the performance Zelter made the following speech: "My dear boy, from this day you are no longer an apprentice, but an independent member of the brotherhood of musicians. I proclaim you independent in the name of Mozart, Haydn, and old father Bach." One birthday gift that Felix received that day was from his grandmother. It was something he always cherished: a copy of the score of the *St. Mathew Passion* by Johann Sebastian Bach.

When Felix was sixteen, he wrote the remarkable piano quartet Op. 3 in B Minor which he dedicated to Goethe. The scherzo movement of this composition was very unusual. Already Felix showed his genius for writing music which had a fairy-like quality. No one had ever written a scherzo that was quite so light and fantastic. If Mendelssohn had written nothing but scherzos, he would have left his mark in music.

At about this time Felix and Fanny had just finished reading a new German translation of Shakespeare's plays. Felix was particularly fond of *A Midsummer Night's Dream*. He composed several compositions based on this play: an overture, a nocturne and a scherzo. When you listen to this music, it is easy to imagine fairies dancing in the air.

For several years after this Felix thought about an idea that he finally carried out when he was twenty. He loved the music of Bach, and he particularly loved the *St. Mathew Passion*. He wanted the people of Berlin to hear this wonderful music. They had not because at this time Bach's music was not often played in Germany. With a great deal of work, Felix got together the singers and the orchestra, and he prepared a fine performance of the *St. Mathew Passion*. It was such a great success that it had to be repeated very soon afterwards. This was the beginning of a revival of interest in Bach's music in Germany. Felix also worked to have a momument to the memory of Bach erected at the threshold of the St. Thomas School in Leipzig.

In 1829, the same year as the performance of the *St. Mathew Passion,* Mendelssohn made his first trip to England. The English people loved his music, and many trips followed. In all, Mendelssohn made ten trips to England during his lifetime.

After Mendelssohn's first concert in England, his *Overture to A Midsummer Night's Dream* was accidentally left in a coach and never found. Mendelssohn, with no difficulty, wrote out another score of the work.

When the first tour through England was over, Mendelssohn and his good friend Klingemann, went to visit Scotland. Mendelssohn was much impressed by the Scottish scenery. He was particularly fascinated by Fingal's Cave. This cave was formed by two tall rocks which made an arch over the sea below. Fingal was a famous giant-hero who was supposed to have been able to step from rock to rock without getting his feet wet. If you listen carefully to Mendelssohn's *The Overture to Fingal's Cave,* sometimes called *Hebrides Overture,* you can hear all the lovely echoes in the music that Mendelssohn must have heard when he visited the cave. The *Scotch Symphony* and a piano piece called *The Scotch Sonata* were also inspired by this trip.

After his return to London, Mendelssohn planned to go to Berlin to attend the wedding of his sister Fanny to the young painter, William Hensel. Unfortunately, he was thrown from a coach and his knee was hurt so badly that he had to remain in his room in London for almost two months. This was a great disappointment, and Mendelssohn tried to forget his bad luck by working on his compositions.

It was at this time that he began to compose his piano pieces *Songs Without Words.* When they were finished, there were forty-nine of them and each piece was given a special name. Some of these names were given by Mendelssohn, but most of them were given by the pianist and composer, Stephen Heller. One very lovely one, Heller called *Spring Song*. Originally, Mendelssohn named it *Camberwell Green* because when he wrote it he was visiting some English friends who lived near Camberwell Green. Here are a few bars of this joyous music:

Another well-known composition of this period is the Piano Concerto in G Minor. In this piece Mendelssohn did several things which were very different. Usually for the beginning of a concerto, a composer writes a rather long part for the orchestra alone in which the themes of the first movement are announced. Then the solo instrument comes in. However, in this concerto the orchestra plays only seven measures of music before the pianist begins. Also, as the piece is played there is no stop between the movements. The first movement goes right into the second, and the second goes right into the third. This had not been done in a concerto before.

Mendelssohn did a great deal of travelling to perform and conduct his compositions. Each country he went to seemed to inspire him with an idea for a new work. When he was twenty, for example, he visited Italy and got the idea for his fourth symphony, the one that has been always called the *Italian Symphony*. And visits to England always inspired new works.

After two more successful trips to England, Mendelssohn accepted the position of General Musical Director in Düsseldorf, Germany. He was not too happy in his work in Düsseldorf because he was not permitted to play the kind of programs he thought the people should hear. He tried to forget this unhappiness by working on a new composition, an oratorio, *St. Paul.* While he was at work he received news of his father's death and went home to comfort his family. On his return to Düsseldorf, he worked hard to finish *St. Paul,* because he wanted it to be known as a tribute to his father.

Sometime after this he was appointed Conductor of the Gewandhaus Concerts in Leipzig, and he left Düsseldorf. The Gewandhaus was a large auditorium, and many important concerts were given there. In Leipzig, Mendelssohn met the famous musicians, Chopin, Schumann, Rossini, and Wagner. He became very friendly with Robert Schumann, and Schumann showed him the Symphony in C Major of Schubert, which he had discovered in Vienna. This symphony, *The Great,* or *The Symphony of Heavenly Lengths,* as Schumann called it, was performed by Mendelssohn at one of the Gewandhaus Concerts.

The most wonderful thing that happened to Mendelssohn in Leipzig was meeting and falling in love with a beautiful girl named Cecile Jean-Renaud. Cecile was eighteen, and Felix was twenty-eight. After being engaged for a few months, they were married in Frankfurt in the spring of 1837. It was a wonderful marriage and five children were born to them: Karl, Marie, Paul, Felix, and Lili. However, not one of them was a musician.

Mendelssohn was especially happy when he could be at home in Leipzig with Cecile and the children. He would play games and romp with the children and once, when Cecile walked into the room, she was horrified to find Mendelssohn teaching Marie the C major scale with the wrong fingering.

Unfortunately Mendelssohn did not have too much time to be at home. Besides his concerts and his work in Leipzig, he was also made head of a new section of the Academy of Arts in Berlin. He accepted this position only to please the King, Frederic William IV of Prussia. In the same year, 1841, he returned to Leipzig and founded the famous Leipzig Conservatory, which is still in existence. Mendelssohn taught piano and composition at the school, and he also invited other important musicians to teach there.

During this time when Mendelssohn was so busy giving concerts and teaching, he was also working on the composition which is probably his most famous one, his oratorio *Elijah*. When it was almost finished, he wrote to the singer Jenny Lind, "I am jumping around my room for joy. If my work turns out half as good as I fancy it is, how pleased I shall be."

The first performance of *Elijah* was given in the town hall at Birmingham, England on August 26, 1846. There was a tremendous audience in the hall, and when Mendelssohn came on the stage to conduct, the applause was deafening. When the performance was finished, the whole audience sprang to its feet in excitement. Mendelssohn was a hero! The following year there were four more performances of *Elijah* in England. Queen Victoria and Prince Albert, who were already good friends of Mendelssohn, were at the second performance. Before Mendelssohn left for Frankfurt, where his family was now living, he spent two hours playing the piano for Queen Victoria and Prince Albert.

The *Elijah* had brought Mendelssohn fame and great honor, but the excitement, in addition to his work, was a little too much for him. He was exhausted and ill. Then, when he had been home only a few days, he received the news of Fanny's sudden death. The shock was such a great one that he fell to the floor unconscious. He recovered a little, but he was never really well again.

During his last illness the whole town of Leipzig was concerned. It was as though a king were ill. Bulletins were given out several times a day, telling of Mendelssohn's condition. Suddenly he took a turn for the worse, and he died quietly on November 4, 1847, at thirty-eight years of age.

The funeral was attended by crowds of musicians, friends, and students. The band played one of his own *Songs Without Words,* which became known as the *Funeral March*. At the close of the service, the choir sang the final chorus from Bach's *St. Mathew Passion*. Mendelssohn's body was then taken to Berlin where he was buried next to his beloved sister, Fanny.

In Leipzig there is a Mendelssohn Monument, and in Frankfurt there is a large tablet above the building where Mendelssohn was born.

Mendelssohn left many beautiful compositions.

Among them are the oratorios *Elijah* and *St. Paul,* five symphonies, chamber music, the well-known Violin Concerto in E Minor, piano music, overtures, and his delightful scherzos.

Frederic Francois Chopin

1810—1849

Frederic Francois Chopin, who was affectionately called Fritsek, was born in the little village of Zelozowa, Poland. This village was about twenty-eight miles west of Warsaw.

The date of Fritsek's birth has always been a puzzle. Fritsek, his mother, and his sisters used to say it was March 1, 1810. Other people claimed that he was born on March 1, 1809. But Fritsek's father insisted that February 22, 1810 was the correct day. This is the date that has been accepted.

Nicolas, Fritsek's father, was a Frenchman who came to Poland when he was seventeen years old. At first he was a bookkeeper in a tobacco plant, but after he had been in Poland for only a short time he became a tutor to the children of the Countess Sharbeck. It was in her house that Nicolas met Justina de Krysanowska, a young lady who was a "poor relation" of the Sharbeck's. He fell in love with Justina, and they were married on June 2, 1806.

The Chopins had four children, Ludwika (Louise), Fryderk Franciszek (Frederic Francois), Isabella, and Emilia. Shortly after Fritsek was born, the family moved to Warsaw because Nicolas became a professor of French at the newly founded Lyceum. This was a school very much like our high school. In order to earn extra money, Nicolas had several of the boys from the school board at his home. Justina Chopin played the piano and gave piano lessons to the boys. She also sang a little. Mr. Chopin played both the violin and the flute.

The Chopins were disappointed in Fritsek when he was an infant because he cried when he heard music. They thought he cried because he did not like it; but they soon discovered that instead he was very sensitive to the sounds, and he cried because he loved it. As soon as Fritsek could walk, he stood close to the piano whenever Ludwika was practicing. When Ludwika started to have piano lessons with the Bohemian musician Adalbert Zywyn, Fritsek, then six, begged to have lessons with him, too.

Zywyn was really a violinist, but he knew a great deal about music and gave Fritsek a good foundation on the piano. He taught the boy many compositions of Bach. Fritsek and his teacher were very good friends. They took long walks together. Zywyn would say, "Always remember, Fritsek, music comes from the songs of simple people." Fritsek always did remember this, and his music is full of Polish folk melodies.

Fritsek also spent a great deal of time improvising on the piano. When he was only seven years old, he composed a Polonaise, that is a Polish dance, which he dedicated to the Countess Victoire Sharbek. Since he had not as yet learned to write music, his teacher, Zywyn, wrote it down for him. The piece was published, and everyone began to speak of Fritsek as a second Mozart.

When Fritsek was eight, he played in public for the first time. His mother had made him a beautiful suit with a large, hand-made, white lace collar. Unfortunately, Mrs. Chopin was ill and could not go to hear her son play, but his father and Master Zywyn did go. Fritsek played beautifully; he already had what was called a "magic touch" on the piano. When he came home after the concert, his mother was most anxious to know what the audience liked best. Fritsek very modestly said, "My collar, mama, my collar."

Fritsek was only ten years old when he composed a *Military March* which he dedicated to the Grand Duke. The Grand Duke was so fond of it that he had it arranged for a military band, and it was played when the soldiers were on parade.

In the midst of all this music, Fritsek was also receiving some sort of an education. He had lessons at home in geography, Latin, and mathematics. When he was thirteen, he entered the fourth class in the Warsaw High School where his father taught French. This was equivalent to our sophomore year in high school. About the same time he had lessons in piano and theory from Joseph Elsner who was the founder and head of the Warsaw Conservatory of Music.

Although Fritsek was never a robust boy, he joined in all the games and amusements of his companions. We even hear of his going skating and cracking his head on the ice. Once, when Fritsek had stayed out in the park later than he should have, he bribed a schoolmate with a bag of candy so that the boy would not tell Mr. Chopin where his son had been.

Beside music, Chopin liked to write plays and act them out. Once when his father had a birthday party, all four Chopin children performed a comedy called *The Mistake* that Fritsek and his sister Emilia had written.

During the school holidays Fritsek loved to go to the country villages and listen to the Polish Folk music. The peasants played and danced the mazurkas, the polonaises, and the krakowiaks. These are all national Polish dances, and many of Fritsek's later compositions were inspired by their melodies.

When Fritsek was fifteen, he played for the Tsar, Alexander, who was so impressed that he gave the boy a diamond ring. It was also in that year that his first important piano piece, a rondo in C Minor, was published.

During Fritsek's last year at school he worked very hard and his health, which was always a problem to him, was affected. His sister, Emilia, also had not been well, and their mother took them both to a health resort known as Bad Reinertz. The night before leaving, Fritsek dashed off a polonaise as a gift to one of his schoolmates. This piece has always been called *Adieu a Wilhelm Kolberg*. After the rest in Bad Reinertz, Fritsek was much better, but Emilia never got well again. A few months later she died of tuberculosis.

When Fritsek returned to Warsaw, he spent all of his time on his compositions. He entered the Warsaw

Conservatory of Music where he continued his studies with Joseph Elsner, who said of him, "The boy has astounding capacity, musical genius."

Fritsek was anxious to travel, and it was a great joy to him when a friend of his father, Dr. Jarochi, announced that he was going to Berlin and offered to take the boy with him. Fritsek looked forward to going to the opera, seeing some plays, and perhaps even meeting some famous musicians. He went to the opera several times and loved it. But when he did see Mendelssohn and Zelker on the street, he was too shy to introduce himself to them.

On the return trip to Warsaw an incident occurred that was long talked about by the people in a small village. The stagecoach in which Dr. Jarochi and Fritsek were travelling had to stop for one hour because the horses had to be changed. While Fritsek and the doctor were waiting, they went into an inn to look around. Fritsek noticed a piano in the corner of one of the rooms. He tried it and, as the instrument was a pretty good one, he began to improvise. He had not realized that all the fellow passengers, the postman, the innkeeper, and several guests had come into the room and were enjoying his playing. Everyone was sorry when the coach was ready and Fritsek had to leave.

Back in Warsaw Fritsek immediately started his lessons with Elsner again. He was more determined than ever to become a fine pianist so that he could travel about and give concerts.

Fritsek had a studio on the top floor of his house and there he practiced for hours and hours. However, he did not shut himself away from the world completely; he also went to dances and evening parties. It was at this time that Fritsek was secretly in love with a lovely young singer at the conservatory, Constantia Gladkowska. She inspired many of Fritsek's compositions, particularly the beautiful slow movement of his Piano Concerto in F Minor. Unfortunately, he never told the young lady of his love, and she later married another.

When Fritsek was nineteen, he had passed all his examinations at the Warsaw Conservatory and was ready to go out into the world and give concerts.

The first city that Fritsek wanted to play in was Vienna, the city of Haydn, Mozart, Beethoven, and Schubert. Before the end of July, 1829, Fritsek set out for Vienna with four of his Warsaw friends who happened also to be going to that city. Fritsek's teacher, Elsner, had given him a letter of introduction to the publisher Haslinger. As soon as they arrived in Vienna, Fritsek went to see Haslinger, who promised to publish some of the young composer's works.

Chopin's first concert in Vienna was a great success. The Viennese had never heard music like Chopin's *Krakowiak Rondo*. Chopin was the first composer to use melodies and rhythms of native Polish folk music in his own music. Krakow, or Cracow, as it is sometimes spelled, was a province in Poland, and the *Krakowiak Rondo* had many of its folk tunes in it.

After a second concert in Vienna, Chopin went back to Warsaw; but not for long, because his next dream was to go to Paris. Since there was great political unrest in Poland and a threat of revolution against the Russian rulers, he decided he had better leave soon.

Chopin's friends gave him a large farewell party, and as a parting gift he was given a silver goblet filled with Polish earth so that he would always remember his native country. Chopin never returned to Poland.

On the way to Paris, Chopin gave concerts in Breslau, Dresden, Prague, Vienna, Munich, and Stuttgart. The tour was not very successful financially, and many times Chopin did not have a penny in his pocket. When he got to Munich, he had to wait until he received some money from his father before he could go on.

The money arrived, and Chopin and his friend, Titus, who was travelling with him, went on to Stuttgart. In Stuttgart news was received that Warsaw had surrendered to the Russians. This upset Chopin very much. He had a strong patriotic feeling and wanted to go back to Poland and help his people. Titus convinced him that his duty to Poland was to compose instead. It was at this time that Chopin wrote his Etude in C Minor, Opus 10, No. 12, which has always been known as the *Revolutionary Étude*.

Chopin finally arrived in Paris in the early autumn of 1831. Paris at this time was the center of literature and music. Chopin met the musicians Cherubini, Bellini, Meyerbeer, Mendelssohn, and Liszt. He also met the great writers Victor Hugo, Balzac, Alexander Dumas, Alfred de Musset, and Heinrich Heine.

Chopin's first concert in Paris was very successful. Mendelssohn and Liszt were in the audience, and it was said that they applauded furiously.

However, life in Paris was not easy for Chopin. He was not able to earn much money. He was so discouraged that he finally thought of going to America to seek his fortune. One day as he was considering this, he met his friend, Prince Radziwill, on the street. The Prince suggested that the young composer come with him to an evening party, or *soiree,* as it was called, at the home of the wealthy Rothschilds. Chopin went along and was asked to play. Everyone was enchanted.

Chopin's playing was more suited to small recitals than to large concert halls, and from that time on he was engaged for many such concerts. Chopin also became the teacher of many of the nobles he first met at the Rothschilds.

It was something new for the aristocracy to find a piano teacher who was not only a fine pianist and a great composer, but also a gentleman, who appeared in beautifully fitted waistcoats and white kid gloves. Chopin was able to ask twenty francs, which was about four dollars, for a lesson; in those days that was considered a great deal of money. Since he gave about six lessons a day, his money troubles were over. During this time Chopin dedicated many of his compositions to princes and princesses.

One of Chopin's good friends, in his early Paris days, was the brilliant pianist, Franz Liszt. He played many of Chopin's compositions, especially his études. Chopin's études, or studies, are different from any études that were written before. Études are usually just exercises to improve the fingers. Chopin's études do this, but each one of the twenty-four he wrote is also a remarkable piece of music. Among them are the *Black Key,* the *Aeolian Harp,* the *Revolutionary,* the *Winter Wind,* and the *Ocean.*

In the *Black Key Étude* Chopin used the thumb on the black keys of the piano for the first time. He also used many other unusual fingerings in his études, and for this reason they were considered revolutionary.

It was about this time that the important composer Robert Schumann heard one of Chopin's piano compositions *Laci darem' Variations.* He said, "Hats off, gentlemen! A genius!"

During the summer of 1835 Chopin's parents, whom

he had not seen for five years, went to Carlsbad for their health. Since Carlsbad was not too far away from Paris, Chopin decided to join them. The reunion was a joyous one. They stayed together for a whole month. This was the last time that Chopin ever saw his parents.

On the way back to Paris, Chopin stopped in Dresden to visit some old friends, the Wodzinskis. The three boys of this family had been schoolmates of Chopin; and Marya, their sister, had been a little girl at that time. Chopin was amazed to see how lovely Marya had become. It was love at first sight. Chopin hoped to marry Marya, but her father would not consent to this. As a parting gift Chopin gave Marya his Waltz in A♭ Major, which has always been known as the *Adieu Waltz*. He went back to Paris brokenhearted.

After Chopin's return to Paris, he was not very well. He had had influenza, and he was also very much upset about his unhappy love affair. He could not get Marya out of his mind. One evening Chopin's friend, Liszt, introduced him to a most unusual woman, a writer. Her real name was Amandine Aurore Lucie Dupin, baronne Dudevent, but she used the name George Sand.

Chopin had never met anyone quite like her before. George Sand wore men's clothes and she smoked big black cigars. She was a very clever woman and well informed in music and all the arts. The two became great friends. They were together constantly.

George Sand's son, Maurice, had been ill, and Mme. Sand was going to take him and her daughter, Solange, on a trip to the island of Majorca, off the coast of Spain. Mme. Sand suggested that Chopin join them, and he gladly accepted. Chopin, too, had not been well, and he thought that the dry warm climate of Majorca would improve his health.

When they arrived in Majorca, George Sand and Chopin found the country beautiful but the living conditions primitive. Their living quarters were in a deserted monastery called Valdemoso. Soon after their arrival Chopin took a long walk, and on the way back he was caught in a terrible rain storm. By the time he had reached Valdemoso, he had a chill and had to go to bed. This was a bad beginning, and to make matters worse, the rain never seemed to stop.

George Sand took good care of Chopin; and on the days that he felt better, he composed some beautiful music. Many of his twenty-four preludes were composed in the monastery at Valdemoso. He also composed polonaises, ballades, and his C♯ Minor Scherzo during this time.

When the weather was good enough to travel again, Mme. Sand, the children, and Chopin left for Nohant. This was Mme. Sand's beautiful home in the outskirts of Paris. There Chopin began to feel better, and he soon finished his B♭ Minor Sonata. The slow movement, a funeral march, was one of Chopin's favorites. Here are a few measures of this sad music:

In the autumn of 1840 Chopin felt well enough to return to Paris and do some teaching. As a teacher he was very patient when the student was attentive and played well. If a pupil played a wrong note, however, he had a violent fit of temper. He was known to break a chair in two and chase the pupil from the room with,

"Get out of here and never show your face again."

Between the years 1839 and 1847 George Sand continued to be a great friend and a real inspiration to Chopin. Then, through some misunderstandings, they parted and never met again.

After this Chopin's health began to fail rapidly, but because he was in need of money, he continued teaching and playing. He gave a concert in Paris on February 16, 1848, and then accepted a concert engagement in London. The London fogs were very bad for Chopin's lungs, and when he returned to Paris, he was so ill nothing could be done for him. He died in Paris on October 17, 1849.

Chopin's funeral was one of great splendor. The Mozart *Requiem* was sung; his own *Funeral March* was played; and two of his beautiful preludes were played on the organ. A small box of Polish earth was sprinkled around his grave in the cemetery of Père-Lachaise. Many pupils and friends came to pay their last respects to the greatest composer of piano music of all times.

Except for some songs, an early trio, and a 'cello sonata, all of Chopin's music was written for the piano or is dominated by the piano. Chopin's piano music is loved by piano students, concert performers, and audiences all over the world. There is hardly a piano recital anywhere that does not have a piece by Chopin on the program.

Johannes Brahms

1833—1897

Johannes Brahms, or Hannes, as he was affectionately called, was born on May 7, 1833 in Hamburg, Germany.

His father, Johann Jakob, ran away from home twice before his parents consented to his becoming a musician. Finally, with his double bass strapped to his back and the good wishes of his parents, Johann Jakob left the sleepy little town of Heide to seek his fortune in Hamburg, the capital of Lower Germany.

When Johann Jakob arrived in Hamburg he worked hard on the double bass and, in order to earn some money, he played in little taverns. His next position was in a band, but he had dreams of playing in a theater orchestra and several years later his dreams came true.

In the meantime Johann Jakob had fallen in love

with Johanna Nissen. They were married on June 9, 1830. Although Johanna was forty-one and Johann twenty-four it was a good marriage. Johanna was a fine wife, and she earned a little extra money as a seamstress.

Three children were born to Johann Jakob and Johanna; Elizabeth, Johannes, and Fritz. Johannes was born in a small dreary apartment at 60 Speckstrasse. This house still stands and looks very much as it did then.

It was fortunate that Hannes loved music because his father was determined that he was going to become a musician. When Hannes was six years old, his father began to teach him the notes. He was pleased that Hannes could name every note struck on the piano, even when he was turned around so that he could not see the keyboard. Mr. Brahms was a little disappointed when Hannes announced that he wanted to become a pianist. His father had hoped he would be a bass player, too. However, Hannes had his way, and when he was seven he was taken to Otto Cossel for piano lessons. Cossel soon recognized Hannes' talent and was delighted with his quick progress.

When Hannes was ten years old, a travelling agent passed through Hamburg and was taken to hear Hannes play the piano. The agent suggested that it would be a good idea for him to take the boy to America, where he could make a great deal of money touring as a child prodigy. Hannes' teacher, Cossel, would not let Mr. Brahms do this because he felt that the boy had to study much more before he could give concerts. To show that his advice was right, he took Hannes to his own teacher, the celebrated musician Eduard Marxen. Marxen was so impressed with

Hannes' ability that he offered to take complete charge of the boy's musical education.

Marxen was a great teacher; he gave Hannes thorough training in the piano and in the theory of music. He gave his pupil many works of Bach and Beethoven to learn. Hannes practiced the piano for hours and hours each day, but he was always thinking about the works he would like to compose. Many years later when he talked about his days with Marxen he often said, "I was always composing my finest songs in the morning when I was cleaning my boots."

He also said that as a child he had had two great loves, and these had remained with him his whole life. One was music, and the other his collection of tin soldiers. Even when he was an old bearded master, he had his tin soldiers and he used to set them up for the children of his landlady, Frau Truxa.

The young Hannes did unusual things when he had his piano lessons with Marxen. Once he transposed many of the Bach preludes and fugues at sight. To *transpose* means to take a piece of music and to play it in a key other than the one in which it is written. This is a difficult thing to do, especially with Bach preludes and fugues.

Not too much is known about the rest of Hannes' education. He did go to two schools. The first one was not a very good one, but in the second one he learned a little French and English besides the usual subjects. Hannes seemed to get most of his education by himself. He was a great reader.

When Hannes was only twelve years old, he had to help earn the family income. At first he gave piano lessons; and then when he was thirteen, he played in cheap music halls. He hated this work, and the late hours were bad for him. Fortunately at this time Adolph Giesmann, a friend of his father, invited him to his country house in Winsen for the whole summer. In exchange, Hannes was to give piano lessons to Giesmann's daughter, Lieschen, who was about his age.

This was a wonderful summer for Hannes. For the first time in his life he enjoyed the beauties of the out-of-doors. Lieschen and he took long walks in the woods, and they hunted for bird's nests and caught butterflies. From that time on Hannes was a great lover of nature, just as his idol Beethoven had been. But all was not play. Marxen had given Hannes much work to do over the summer, and the boy finished it all. Hannes returned to Hamburg healthier and happier than he had ever been. He was already impatient for the following summer to arrive because he had been invited to return to Winsen.

By the time the next summer had arrived and Hannes was ready to go back to Winsen, everyone in Winsen knew what a fine musician he was. He was invited to give little concerts in the homes of the best families. He even organized the "Winsen Male Choir" and composed several songs for them. One was a four part song on the letters of the alphabet *A.B.C.* The other was called *Postilion's Morgenlied* (*Postilion's Morning Song*).

When summer was over and Hannes went back to Hamburg, he gave his first public concert. The next year, when he was sixteen, he gave his second. This concert was really a great success. He played, among other things, Beethoven's *Waldstein Sonata* and a fantasy of his own which was based on a favorite waltz theme of the day. All these early compositions of Brahms have disappeared.

In 1851 when Brahms was eighteen, he met the Hungarian violinist Eduard Remenyi. His gypsy-like way of playing the violin fascinated Brahms. This was the first time that Brahms had heard the Gypsy and Hungarian folk tunes, and he was very much influenced by them. He later composed four sets of *Hungarian Dances* for piano duet, which he also arranged for piano solo and for orchestra.

Here are a few measures of the one in F♯ minor:

Among Brahms' other compositions that were influenced by Gypsy folk tunes are a set of eleven songs known as the *Zigeunelieder* (*Gypsy Songs*) and the last movement of his Piano Quartet in C Minor, known as *Rondo alla Zingarese* (*Gypsy Rondo*).

Soon after they became friends, Brahms and Remenyi went on a little concert tour. Their first concert was in Winsen, where Johannes was already known. Then they played in a little town called Celle.

The piano in the concert hall in Celle was tuned one half tone below what it should be, so that when the note C was struck, B came out instead. It was very difficult for Remenyi to tune his violin one half step down, so Brahms transposed at sight the Beethoven C Minor Violin and Piano Sonata to C♯ minor, one half step up. In this way the piece sounded as if it were being played in C minor, the key in which Remenyi was also playing. Remenyi, as well as the audience, was amazed!

When Brahms and Remenyi arrived in Hanover, Remenyi took Brahms to meet the great violinist of the day, Joseph Joachim. Brahms played some of his compositions, and Joachim was spellbound. He immediately arranged for Brahms and Remenyi to play for the King of Hanover. Then Joachim wrote a glowing account of Brahms' work to the important composer, Robert Schumann, and to the "King of Pianists," Franz Liszt. Joachim offered to help Brahms at any time that he might need help. It was not only Brahms' gift for music that impressed Joachim, it was also the fact that Brahms was a modest and pleasant young man. At that time he had fair smooth skin and flowing blond hair. It is difficult for us to imagine Brahms looking like this because most of the pictures we see of him show a long beard.

Remenyi now became jealous of all the attention given to Brahms and quarreled with him. The two soon parted. At first Brahms felt completely stranded, but then he remembered the kind words of Joachim and went to see him. Joachim suggested that Brahms go to visit the Schumann's in Düsseldorf because Robert Schumann had a great deal of influence, and Clara Schumann was a marvellous pianist who would certainly play the young composer's sonatas at her concerts. Brahms followed Joachim's advice, and an important and wonderful friendship began.

Schumann was most enthusiastic about Brahm's compositions. He called Brahms "The Young Eagle." He also wrote an article in which he called Brahms one of the great geniuses of the time. Besides this Schumann introduced Brahms to the music publishers Breitkopf and Härtel. They became the composer's first publishers.

It was just eight months since Johannes left Hamburg; he had come a long way in that short time. But now he wanted most of all to go home for the Christmas holidays. He went, and there was much rejoicing in Hamburg. Hannes was treated like a hero. After the New Year he set off for Hanover where Joachim and the Schumanns were spending some time. Shortly after Brahms arrived, Schumann became very ill and had to be sent to a sanatorium. He never recovered, and he died on July 27, 1856.

Brahms helped Clara Schumann very much during the trying days that followed. He became one of the family, and the children loved him. About this time he wrote a book of charming children's folk songs for the Schumann children. Clara was soon able to continue her teaching and her concerts, but she never forgot Johannes' help. They were friends for the rest of their lives.

When Johannes was twenty-four, he was engaged as Director of the Court Concerts and of the Choral Society of Lippe-Detmold.

This was a small town, but a beautiful one. Brahms had the lovely countryside to walk in, and his work was most enjoyable. He conducted the chorus; he played at the court concerts; and he taught the piano to Princess Friederike. Since he did not have to be in Detmold constantly, he was able to spend a great deal of time on his compositions. One of his important works in this period was the Piano Concerto in D Minor. This piece was not well received when it was first played, because Brahms had written it in a new way. He had made the piano part sound like part of the orchestra. In concertos before this, the piano part had always been written to show off the pianist. Many years passed before this piece was really appreciated.

After almost three years in Detmold, Brahms went back to Hamburg. There he became head of the Hamburg Ladies' Choir, but he spent most of his time composing. Here his reputation as a composer grew constantly until he finally felt that the time had come for him to go to Vienna, the city of Haydn, Mozart, Beethoven, and Schubert.

Brahms arrived in Vienna in September of 1862, and from that time on, except for summers spent in Baden-Baden, Ischl, and Thün, Vienna was his home.

The first person Brahms visited in Vienna was Bertha Faber. She had been in the Hamburg Ladies' Choir, and at one time Brahms had thought he was in love with her. Now she was married and had recently had her first child. Brahms had a gift for the baby. It was the beautiful song *Wiegenlied* (*Cradle Song*). This piece has become one of the best loved of Brahms' little compositions.

Brahms made many friends in Vienna. He had many musical evenings in his apartment, and it was there that some of his music was played for the first time. Beside music, Brahms was also able to talk on almost any subject because he had always read widely. He used to say, "Whoever wishes to play well, must not only practice a great deal but read many books."

In September of 1863 Brahms was made Director of the "Singakademie" ("Academy of Singing") in Vienna. He was not too happy in this position, and the following year he resigned. In the year that he was director, he composed his important *German Requiem*. This was performed at the Cathedral in Bremen on Good Friday, April 10, 1868, with Brahms conducting. The Cathedral was full to the doors, and all of Brahms' friends were there, including Clara Schumann, who had travelled a great distance to be present.

It was a magnificent performance, and from that

day on Brahms was accepted as a great master. Other well-known compositions that Brahms composed about this time were: a set of songs written for a quartet of singers, a piano duet known as the *Liebeslieder Waltzes,* and the lovely Waltzes Op. 39 for Piano Duet. Brahms arranged one of the Waltzes Op. 39 for piano solo and it is popularly known as *The Waltz in A♭*, although the original was in A.

Here are a few bars:

Brahms was forty-two years old at the time his first symphony, the Symphony in C Minor, was finished. When someone asked him why he waited so long to write a symphony, he modestly said, "How can I write a symphony when I feel the shadow of the great Beethoven treading constantly behind me." In later years Brahms wrote three more symphonies. The second one is in D major, the third is in F major, and the fourth is in E minor. All four are masterpieces, and all are performed by orchestras everywhere.

In 1879, Brahms was given the honorary degree of Doctor of Philosophy by the University of Breslau. For that occasion he wrote his well-known *Academic Festival Overture*. The beautiful *Double Concerto* for 'cello, violin and orchestra, the Violin Concerto in D Major and the Second Piano Concerto in B♭ Major were composed about this time, also.

Brahms never married, although he was in love several times. When a woman once asked him why he never married, he said, "None of them would have me; and if there had been one who would, I could not have stood her on account of her bad taste."

Brahms adored children, and children loved him. He always stopped to play with them, and they knew that in his pockets were sweets just for them. They ran to greet him whenever they heard that the "little round gentleman with the long beard and the big cigar" was around.

Some people gave Brahms the nickname of "gruff bear," but he really was a kind and lonely man and he only pretended to be gruff. Brahms was also very witty. Once a 'cellist who was playing with him said, "Master, you are playing so loudly that I can hardly hear myself." Brahms replied, "Happy man." Another time a composer showed Brahms one of his new compositions. It was a long piece and not a very good one and after Brahms had examined it carefully, all he could say was, "Tell me, young man, where do you get your beautiful manuscript paper?"

As a composer, Brahms did not invent any new forms. He continued on where Beethoven left off. Some people have even said that Brahms' First Symphony could have been Beethoven's tenth. Brahms' melodies are beautiful; his rhythms are powerful. Once you have heard a Brahms' rhythm, you will always remember it. Another very important part of Brahms' works are his songs. Next to Schubert, Brahms was the greatest German *lieder* composer.

The last compositions of Brahms were his *Four Serious Songs* and his eleven organ preludes. Just as he was completing the songs, he received the news that his friend Clara Schumann had died. It was almost as if Brahms knew what was to happen because in the songs death is mentioned several times.

When Brahms was returning home from Clara's funeral, he suddenly felt quite ill. The shock of Clara's death was a great one; and even though he lived for almost a year after, he was never well again.

Brahms died April 3, 1897, a month and four days before his sixty-fourth birthday. Many people came to his funeral, and he was given a grave near Beethoven and Schubert.

In many German cities there have been monuments erected in Brahms' memory. There are special memorial tablets in the house in Hamburg where he was born, in the house in Vienna where he spent his last days, and in the houses in Ischl and Thün where he spent his summers.

Among the great works that Brahms left are: four symphonies, overtures, piano works, violin and 'cello works, chamber music, organ works, choral works, and the wonderful *lieder*.

Antonin Leopold Dvořák

1841—1904

Antonin Leopold Dvořák, many times just called Anton Dvořák, was born in the small Bohemian village of Nelahozeves on September 8, 1841.

Antonin's father, František, was the proprietor of the village inn and was also the village butcher. František was a musical man; he played the violin, the zither, and he also sang Bohemian folk songs to entertain his patrons at the inn.

Many of the Bohemian people, later known as the Czechoslovakians, were very musical. The people of Nelahozeves often dressed up in their native costumes and sang and danced on the village green. The lovely music of the polkas and the furiants was played by bands of strolling musicians who came either from Prague or the neighboring villages. Antonin loved to listen to these folk melodies.

Antonin was the eldest and the most musical of the eight children in the large Dvořák family. When he was eight years old, he went to the village school. Along with his regular studies, Antonin studied the violin with the schoolmaster, Josef Spitz. Before long, he played well enough to sit next to his father in the village band. Unfortunately any interesting facts about Antonin's early training have been lost because the old schoolhouse burnt down in 1885.

Antonin's father encouraged his music lessons, but did not want him to be a professional musician. He wanted his son to become a butcher.

When Antonin was twelve years old, he was invited by an uncle, who lived in Zlonice, to come and live with him and his wife. Antonin's parents agreed to this, and the boy went off. This worked out well because the schoolmaster and organist of Zlonice, Anton Liehmann, was an excellent musician. Antonin studied organ, piano, viola, musical theory, and German with him. Liehmann was greatly impressed with Antonin's progress, and the boy loved his master.

The following year Antonin's family came to live in Zlonice because Mr. Dvořák had become the proprietor of the Big Inn. Unfortunately, business did not go very well, and Antonin had to go to work as a butcher's apprentice to help out the family. He had little time for his music; but whenever he could, he played the violin in the village orchestra. Antonin's greatest wish was to become a musician. His father still did not approve of the idea.

At last, to impress his father with his musical ability, Antonin secretly composed a polka. A few of his friends got together and without one rehearsal, they played Antonin's composition for Mr. Dvořák. Unfortunately, Antonin did not know that the trumpet, one of the instruments that he had used, is a transposing instrument. This means that when a trumpeter blows the written note D, for example, the note that comes out is a C. In order for the trumpet to play in the same key as the other instruments, Antonin should have written the notes differently. No wonder Antonin's father said, "But it doesn't make sense." However, this incident did prove to Mr. Dvořák how much Antonin wanted to become a musician.

It was finally decided that Antonin would go to the Organ School in Prague. The exciting day arrived, and father and son piled into the haycart of the peasant, Veselý, and were driven to the great city. It was about forty-five miles from Zlonice, and the roads were bumpy ones. But Antonin did not mind the rough trip. He was full of joy at the thought of becoming a student at such a fine school. The Organ School at Prague was said to be the "nursery" of Czech composers.

At school Antonin worked very hard. He studied the organ, the theory of music, and singing; and he badly needed a piano for his studies. But he was living with relatives who did not have one. Fortunately one of his good friends at school, Karel Bendl, who later became a well-known composer, let him use his instrument. Karel also showed Antonin musical scores by great composers. These opened up a whole new world for the young musician.

After two years, Antonin, now eighteen, was graduated from the Organ School in Prague. He now had to find some way of earning a living and was happy to be accepted as a viola player in the popular Komzák Orchestra. His only problems were that the orchestra did not play very good music and he did not receive very much money for his work. Once when he wanted to hear the performance of a Weber Opera, called *Der Freischutz,* and he had no money with which to buy a ticket, he slipped into the orchestra pit and hid behind the drums.

After a time, the Komzák Orchestra became part of the new Czechish National Theater Orchestra, with the important Czechish musician, Bedřich Smetana, as its conductor. Smetana was known as The Father of Bohemian Music, and his work was soon a great inspiration to Antonin.

For a long time after he began playing with the orchestra, Antonin had no piano. Then finally several of the orchestra players who had a piano invited him to share their apartment. Antonin began at once to compose much music, but he also destroyed a good deal of it. He used to say that he was never cold in those days because he had plenty of "paper" for the fire. The apartment of Antonin and his friends was a small one, and in order for Antonin to get things out of the way, he stuffed some of his compositions into drawers and forgot about them. Because of this, two well-known works were saved from the "fire," a Symphony in C Minor, known as *The Bells of Zlonice* and a set of songs called *The Cypress.*

Antonin had always been anxious to compose an opera, and when he was twenty-nine he wrote one called *Alfred.* This work was not very successful, and, although Antonin wrote ten operas in his lifetime, they are not considered his best works. However, the opera

Rusalka is a very popular one in Prague.

In 1873 Dvořák composed a piece called *Hymnus*. It was with this work that he began to be recognized. The *Hymnus* was a patriotic hymn of praise written for mixed chorus and orchestra to honor the memory of the brave defenders of Bohemia at the Battle of the White Mountain in 1620. It was based on a poem called "The Heirs of the White Mountain." The first performance of the *Hymnus* was on March 9, 1873, and it was a very successful one. The most important result of the performance to Dvořák was that the parents of Anna Cermakova, a young lady with whom he had been in love for several years, gave their permission for a marriage.

Anna and Antonin were married in Prague on November 17, 1873. Not only did Anna make a fine wife, but she was also a musician. She had a lovely contralto voice and sang in the chorus of the National Theatre.

Soon after their marriage, Anna encouraged Antonin to leave the orchestra and become the organist at the Church of St. Adalbert. This was a fine move because it gave him more time to teach and also left his evenings free for composing. The Dvořáks were soon able to have their own home, and in the years to come they had a family of six children. Not one of the children was a professional musician, but they all loved music. One of the daughters married a composer, Josef Suk, who was a pupil of Dvořák.

In the first few years after his marriage, Dvořák composed chamber music, an opera, and several symphonies. Some of them were played, but none of them were published. Then Anna heard about a contest to be held in Vienna for composers. The one who wrote the best original composition would receive money from the State. She insisted that Antonin send one of his works, and he sent his E♭ Major Symphony. Antonin's symphony won first prize.

One of the judges for this competition was the composer, Johannes Brahms. He was very excited about Dvořák's Symphony and was anxious to meet Dvořák. When they did meet, a great friendship began and Brahms did much to help Dvořák. He even wrote to his own publisher, Simrock, and persuaded him to publish some of Dvořák's music. The first piece published was *Moravian Duets.* It appeared under the title *Airs from Moravia.* With these songs, the German musical world took notice of Dvořák for the first time.

Happy with his first prize, Dvořák tried again, and in March, 1875, he won a prize for his Quintet in G Major. However, it was still the *Moravian Duets* that was the best known of his compositions.

The next work of Dvořák that became popular was a group of piano duets called *Slavonic Dances.* These dances became as popular as Brahms' *Hungarian Dances.*

In 1876 the Dvořáks suffered the sudden death of their eldest daughter. In memory of her, Dvořák composed an oratorio called *Stabat Mater.* These words mean *The Mother Stood,* and they are the words which begin a Latin hymn on the Crucifixion. This was the first modern Czechish oratorio. It was first performed in Prague on December 23, 1880, but a performance in England three years later really brought fame to the composer.

The success that was now coming to Dvořák did not spoil him. He was a simple man, and he loved the quiet of his home and his family. He also had a hobby that he loved very much. Just as Johannes Brahms loved his tin soldiers, so Dvořák loved trains. But Dvořák loved real trains. Every morning he took a walk to the Franz Josef railway station, which was not too far away from his home, to study the different engines. He would write down the numbers of each of the locomotives so as not to forget them. Years later, when Dvořák was in America, it was said that he took an hour's drive from his home just to see the Chicago Express thunder by!

Dvořák's *Slavonic Dances* had become so popular that his publishers kept after him for similar works. So he composed a set of songs called *Seven Gypsy Melodies*. The song of this set that has become the most popular is *Songs My Mother Taught Me*. It is a beautiful song and a very good example of Dvořák's lovely simple folk style.

The fame of Antonin Dvořák spread until he was asked to visit other countries. On one of his English trips he took with him a new symphony, his Fourth, in G major. This one was so well liked that an English publisher published it; it has always been known as *The English Symphony*. During this trip Dvořák's *Stabat Mater* received a sensational performance. There were more than eight hundred voices in the chorus.

After this successful English trip Dvořák and his wife were able to buy a house and some land in a country village called Vysoka. The house and garden were simple, but the surrounding hills and forest were beautiful. Dvořák loved to take long walks in the country, and when he got tired he would stop in the village and talk to the farmers and the miners.

By this time many honors had been bestowed on Dvořák. He had been appointed Professor of Composition at the Prague Conservatory. He had won the state prize in Vienna five times. He had been given the degree of Doctor of Philosophy at the Czech University in Prague, and he had been made an honorary Musical Doctor at Cambridge University in England.

Before Dvořák's fiftieth birthday there was still another honor in store for him. He was invited to become the director of the newly opened National Conservatory in New York City. America seemed far away, but the offer was a tempting one. The founder of the school, a wealthy music lover, Mrs. Jeannette Thurber, offered Dvořák $15,000 a year if he would come to America. So much money for one year's work was unheard of in Bohemia. He accepted with the understanding that his teaching was to begin in the fall of 1892. He was given a leave from the Prague Conservatory, and there was much planning and excitement in the Dvořák household.

On September 17, 1892 Dvořák, his wife, two of their six children, and a young man, Joseph Kovařích, who proved to be a valuable friend, sailed from Southampton, England, for America.

Dvořák was well pleased with the Conservatory. He enjoyed his teaching, and his original methods made him a great teacher. He also loved the American folk tunes, especially the Negro spirituals. He tried to impress his American pupils with the idea that they, too, had wonderful folk music and that it should be used.

In the summer of Dvořák's first year in America, he and his family went to Spillville, Iowa. The father of Joseph Kovařích lived here. The town was like a little bit of Bohemia transplanted to America. Dvořák was happy here and especially so because his other four children had arrived and the whole family was together again.

When Dvořák had been in Spillville only a few days,

he began to compose his Quartet in F Major, Opus 96, which has become known as *The American Quartet*. In six days the quartet was finished and everyone was anxious to hear it. A quartet of players consisting of Dvořák playing first violin, Papa Kovařích, second violin, Dvořák's daughter, viola, and his son, the 'cello, played the piece for the first time. Everyone who heard it loved it, as people still do today. It is performed by chamber music groups all over the world.

The people in Spillville never forgot Dvořák's memorable visit. Later, in a spot Dvořák had especially loved, they erected a simple monument to him. Twenty-five years after his death, they named a road after him. It is called the "Dvořák Highway."

On the way back to New York, after the lovely Spillville summer, the Dvořáks stopped to see Niagara Falls. This great sight impressed Dvořák so much that he immediately wrote some themes in his sketch book. These later became a set of eight "humoresques" for piano. The seventh one of the set, the one in G♭ major, has become one of Dvořák's most popular pieces. It has been arranged for many different instruments and is played all over the world.

Here are a few bars of the original piano piece called *Humoresque:*

Back in New York, Dvořák continued his work at the Conservatory. His *Symphony From the New World,* inspired by American folk themes, was performed before an enthusiastic audience at Carnegie Hall on December 15, 1893.

At the end of that year, the family went back to Bohemia, but only with the promise to Mrs. Thurber that they would return the following year. When the family arrived in Prague, they were greeted by crowds of people, gathered in the streets. From everywhere people shouted, "Long live Dvořák!" The composer was truly loved in his native country.

The year at home went by quickly. Dvořák's new compositions were enthusiastically received in Prague, his teaching was good, and before he knew it, it was time to go back to America. His wife and son, Otokar, joined him on this trip.

Somehow, during the third year in America, Dvořák was more lonely than he had been before for Bohemia. He was asked to come back to America for still another year, but he refused. During this last trip to America he composed only one important work, his 'Cello Concerto in B Minor.

On April 16, 1895, Dvořák, his wife, and his son, Otokar, sailed for home. Dvořák's last years were spent at the Prague Conservatory. In 1901 he was appointed head of the school. There he was always surrounded by faithful pupils who followed his teachings gratefully.

Although Dvořák had not been seriously ill, for some time he had not been really well and quite suddenly, on May 1, 1904, he died. He had had a happy life, and he had many friends. His funeral, on May 5, was attended by thousands of people, and heading the procession was the governor of Prague.

Besides Dvořák's popular symphony *From the New World,* the composer had written eight others. He also had composed many symphonic poems for orchestra. A *symphonic poem* is music that expresses a story through sound. A few well-known ones are *The Water-sprite, The Midday Witch, The Golden Spinning Wheel* and *The Wood Dove*. In addition he had written a 'cello concerto, a violin concerto, piano pieces, operas, and songs.

Dvořák's lovely melodies are full of his patriotic feelings for his country. He has sometimes been called The Second Father of Bohemian Music.

Peter Ilich Tchaikowsky

1840—1893

Peter Ilich Tchaikowsky, or Petya, as he was called, was born in Votkinsk, Russia, on May 7, 1840.

The Tchaikowsky family was not a particularly musical one, so Petya's talent was not hereditary. However, the family enjoyed music, and Petya's mother played the piano and sang a little. When Petya was born, his father was an inspector of government mines in Votkinsk, and the family lived in a beautiful, large house. Petya had an older brother, Nicolas, three younger brothers, Hippolytus, Anatole, and Modeste, and a sister, Alexandra.

When Petya was only four and a half years old, his brother Nicholas and a cousin Lydia, who was living with the family at the time, were given piano lessons by the governess, Fanny Durbach. Petya begged and begged for lessons, and finally the governess gave them to him.

The piano was Petya's great love, and he played for hours and hours. Mr. Tchaikowsky saw this and did not want his son to become a musician. One day he said, "Tell me, Son, what would you rather be, a lawyer or an engineer, rich and important, or a poor, starving musician." Petya promptly replied, "I will be a musician." Needless to say, his father hoped that this would never be.

As a child, Petya did not hear much music. He was especially delighted then when his father brought him a music box from St. Petersburg. The music box played an aria from Mozart's opera *Don Giovanni*. Petya played the piece over and over again, and perhaps this was the beginning of his great love for the music of Mozart. Many years later Petya took some themes from Mozart's music that were not very well-known and used them in a suite called *Mozartiana.*

Petya's parents finally realized how much their boy really loved music, and they engaged a special teacher to give him piano lessons. Maria Markovna Patchikov was a fine teacher, but Petya did not study with her for very long. Mr. Tchaikowsky was given a new position in St. Petersburg, and the family had to move.

As soon as the family was settled in its new home, Petya, now eight, was sent to a boarding school. He was unhappy at school, for he missed the loving care that his mother had given him. The only thing that he enjoyed at this time were his piano lessons with his teacher, Philipov.

Eventually Petya became quite ill at school, and it was only after he was home again that he seemed to be better. By this time his father had decided that his son would study to become a lawyer. Although Petya was only ten years old, he was sent to the Preparatory School of Jurisprudence. The boy did fairly well at this school, but he still had dreams of becoming a musician. He joined the choral class at school, and he also studied the piano.

When Petya was fourteen, his mother died suddenly of cholera. The shock was a great one to Petya and all his family. But when they moved in with Mr. Tchaikowsky's brother, Peter, there were young cousins around that helped them all become a little more cheerful. Petya became a great favorite with his cousins and their friends because he improvized waltzes and polkas at the piano.

Petya finished his law studies and graduated from the School of Jurisprudence at nineteen. After graduation he received the position of an official of the first division in the Ministry of Justice. But Petya was not interested in this work and there are many stories told about his absentmindedness. Once, when he was sent from one part of the ministry to another to deliver an important document, he stopped to talk to a friend. During the conversation, not at all realizing what he was doing, he chewed up a good part of the state document. Fortunately, he was able to make another copy of it.

There were not many concerts where the works of great classic composers were played in St. Petersburg at this time. In fact it was even difficult to get hold of the music itself. It has been said that when Petya was twenty-one years old he did not even know how many symphonies Beethoven had written. What he did know, however, was that he was going to be a good musician and that nothing would stand in his way.

Petya soon entered the Conservatory at St. Petersburg, where he studied composition with Zaremba and music orchestration with Anton Rubinstein. Petya worked hard at school, and then during the summer he wrote an overture called *The Storm*. Since he was shy, he asked his friend, Hermann Laroche, to take the piece to Rubinstein. The teacher looked at the way Petya had orchestrated the overture and a "storm" broke loose. Petya had not followed the rules he had learned; he had made up his own.

The young composer continued his studies, and when he was twenty-five years old he received his diploma from the Conservatory at St. Petersburg. He also received a silver medal for a cantata that he had written.

In 1866 Nicholas Rubinstein, Anton's brother, founded a conservatory in Moscow. Tchaikowsky was chosen to be the theory teacher, and on January 17, 1866 he left for Moscow. Nicholas Rubinstein was a wonderful friend in many ways. He gave the new teacher a room in his house, bought him new clothes and introduced him to several young men at the Conservatory who became his friends. Among them were Jurgenson, who became Tchaikowsky's publisher, and Kashkin, who later wrote a biography of Tchaikowsky.

Beside his teaching, Petya also composed. When he wrote his first symphony, called *Winter Day Dreams,* he sent it to Zaremba and Rubinstein. They sent the symphony back with many criticisms. At first Petya was discouraged, but he did not give up. He continued working on the symphony. Two years later, when the piece was played in Moscow for the first time, it was greatly appreciated.

It was at this time that Petya composed his first opera

Voyeveda. He was not pleased with it when it was finished, and he destroyed all of it except the overture and a few of the dances. In the years to come Tchaikowsky composed eleven operas, but only two of them have become well-known. They are *Eugene Onegin* and *The Queen of Spades.*

Tchaikowsky worked hard at his teaching all winter in the Conservatory; but when summer came, he went to the country home of his sister, Alexandra Davidoff. During one of these visits, in the summer of 1871, Tchaikowsky heard the gardener sing a folk tune that fascinated him. This tune became the theme of the second movement of his String Quartet Number One in D Major. This second movement is known as Tchaikowsky's *Andante Cantabile.* It is as popular as Handel's *Largo.*

In one of Tchaikowsky's visits to St. Petersburg, he met the famous "Five." They were a group of young Russian composers, consisting of Balakirev, Cui, Borodin, Moussorgsky, and Rimsky-Korsakov. These composers were especially interested in Russian folk music and were known as the "Nationalistic Composers." When Tchaikowsky composed his second symphony, he was influenced by the ideas of the "Five." Because of the folk tunes in his second symphony, the work is always known as *The Little Russian.* Tchaikowsky became especially friendly with Balakirev and dedicated his beautiful overture *Romeo and Juliette* to him.

Tchaikowsky's next important composition was the Piano Concerto Number 1 in B♭ Minor. This has become one of his most popular pieces. Here are a few notes from the beginning of this exciting work:

In the year 1877, when Tchaikowsky was thirty-seven years old, he hastily married a young lady whom he hardly knew. This brought him great unhappiness. She was not at all suited to his sensitive, high-strung nature, and the marriage actually soon made him ill. He fled to Moscow and then to St. Petersburg. The doctors ordered a rest, and his brother Modeste took him to Switzerland and then to Italy. The peaceful life there did much to help Tchaikowsky regain his health.

At about the same time, Tchaikowsky had a composition student who was also a violinist. The young boy was often engaged to play at the home of the very wealthy widow, Mme. Nadezhda von Meck. The boy told her about his great master, Tchaikowsky, and spoke of how wonderful it would be if the master could only compose and not have to teach. Because she was already a great admirer of Tchaikowsky's compositions, Mme. von Meck decided to help. At first she asked the composer to arrange some of his works for her, and she paid him well. Then she offered him a yearly allowance, but only on the condition that they never meet. Their entire friendship, which lasted almost fourteen years, was carried on by letters. Mme. von Meck was the most unusual patroness music has ever had.

Now that Tchaikowsky had no more money worries, he was able to compose to his heart's content. He finished his opera *Eugene Onegin;* he wrote his Fourth Symphony and dedicated it to "My best friend, Mme. von Meck"; and he wrote his Violin Concerto in D Major. In 1880 he composed the *1812 Overture.* This overture had its first performance at a celebration in the Cathedral in the Kremlin, built in 1812.

Tchaikowsky's reputation as a composer was growing rapidly. He was known in England, France, and America. He had become the fine musician he had dreamed of being.

And then another dream came true. He was able to purchase a country home near Klin. Klin was a town between St. Petersburg and Moscow. In the next few years, he changed his first house for a second, smaller one; but this, too, was in Klin. He loved the country there, and he took long walks in the woods every day. He was given the nickname "The Hermit of Klin."

In addition to composing, Tchaikowsky also spent time conducting his own compositions. His first tour as a conductor was made in 1887. He appeared in Leipzig, Berlin, Prague, Hamburg, Paris, and London.

Even though these concerts were very successful, he was lonely all the time he was gone from home. He wrote to his friend Mme. von Meck, "but would it not be better to stay at home and work . . . I regret that I am not left in peace in the solitude of the country."

When the tour was over, he was happy to be back in his quiet home again. This time his letter to Mme. von Meck was more cheerful: "What a pleasure it has been to watch my flowers grow . . . When I am quite old and past composing, I shall devote myself to growing flowers."

The peaceful life did not last long, however. Tchaikowsky soon left for a second tour. This time he went to Cologne, Frankfurt, Dresden, Geneva, and Hamburg. In Hamburg he met Brahms. He liked Brahms, but he did not like his music. This is easy to understand because Tchaikowsky composed music that is melodic, flowing and very emotional. Brahms' music is beautiful, but it is music that is carefully controlled and thought out. This kind of music is called *intellectual music*.

When Tchaikowsky returned from his second tour in December, 1890, he found a very upsetting letter from Mme. von Meck. In the letter Mme. von Meck told him that she would not be able to continue sending him the yearly allowance because she had lost a great deal of her money. Tchaikowsky wrote to Mme. von Meck, telling her that it would make him happy only to continue writing to her, but Mme. von Meck never answered his letter.

Tchaikowsky tried to forget his unhappiness by immediately setting to work on a new composition, his charming ballet *The Nutcracker*. No sooner had he started, when he received an invitation to come to America. Tchaikowsky was asked to conduct the opening concert at the great new Carnegie Hall. He went and his music was received with enthusiasm. He conducted four concerts in New York, one in Baltimore, and one in Philadelphia. Everywhere the B♭ Minor Piano Concerto, then, as now, was the great favorite.

Tchaikowsky had a good time in America, but when the tour was over, he was happy to be back in his little country home in Klin. He immediately went back to work again on the *Nutcracker Ballet*. Today the concert version, known as *The Nutcracker Suite* is one of the most beloved of Tchaikowsky's works. The music tells of a little girl, Mary, who dreams on Christmas night that her Puppet, the "Nutcracker," comes to life and becomes the leader of a band of lead soldiers against the Mouse King. The little girl slays the Mouse King with her slipper, and the Nutcracker immediately becomes a handsome prince. He carries the little girl off to the Sugar Plum Kingdom where toys and sweetmeats come to life and join in celebrating the happiness of the little girl and her Prince Charming. In the music there is an *Overture*, a *March*, *The Dance of the Sugar Plum Fairy*, a *Russian Dance*, an *Arabian Dance*, a *Chinese Dance*, the fairy like *Dance of the Reed Pipes* and the *Waltz of the Flowers*. In *The Dance of the Sugar Plum Fairy*, Tchaikowsky used an instrument that had never been used in an orchestra before, the celesta. It is a small keyboard instrument with a bell-like tone.

This is a little of the music of *The Sugar Plum Fairy:*

Tchaikowsky's last work was his Symphony Number 6, the *Pathetique*. Tchaikowsky himself said, "Without exaggeration I have put my whole soul into this work."

Tchaikowsky's last concert tour, in June, 1893, brought him to England, where he received the degree of Doctor of Music from the University of Cambridge. After that he went to St. Petersburg to conduct a performance of his *Pathetique*. The first performance of this work was not a very good one, and, unfortunately, Tchaikowsky never heard the thrilling performance given in St. Petersburg only a few weeks later. Several days before the performance, he drank a glass of water that had not been boiled. There was an epidemic of cholera in St. Petersburg and no water was safe unless it had been boiled. In a few days Tchaikowsky was dying of cholera and nothing could be done for him. He died on November 6, 1893, at the age of 53. His favorite brother, Modeste, and his nephew, Vladimir Davidoff, were with him at the end.

Many people came to pay their respects to the great composer. He was buried in the Alexander Nevsky Cemetery in St. Petersburg. His country house in Klin has become The Tchaikowsky Museum.

Among Tchaikowsky's many compositions are symphonies, overtures, ballets, three concertos for piano, a violin concerto, 'cello works, chamber music, songs, and operas.

Not very long ago a Russian composer, Semyon Bogatyryev, who is now living in Moscow, put together from Tchaikowsky's sketches for a seventh symphony, a work known as the *Tchaikowsky Symphony, Number Seven.* Tchaikowsky had left one finished movement, and Bogatyryev wrote the remaining three movements of the symphony, using sketches he found in The Tchaikowsky Museum at Klin.

This symphony had its first performance in the United States in Philadelphia, by the Philadelphia Orchestra, on February 17, 1962.

Sir Edward William Elgar

1857—1934

Sir Edward William Elgar was born on June 2, 1857, in the village of Broadheath, Worcester, England. He is called *Sir* because he was knighted in 1904 by King Edward VII.

The small village of Broadheath was a beautiful one, and although the Elgars moved to Worcester when Edward was only four years old, he had wonderful memories of his birthplace.

Many years later, when he wrote the *Nursery Suite,* for Princess Elizabeth, now Queen Elizabeth, and her sister, Princess Margaret, he remembered a scene from his little village. In one of the pieces of the suite, called

The Wagon Passes, it is easy to imagine a little old man driving a wagon over the many holes in the road at Broadheath. In order to keep his mind off the jerky road, the little old man whistled a tune. The tune was not a very important one, but Edward was fond of it, and he used it in *The Wagon Passes.*

Edward's father, William Henry Elgar, was active in the musical world of Worcester. He was the organist of the Roman Catholic Church of St. George, he played the violin and the piano, and he also owned a music shop.

From the time Edward was a small boy, music was always played in the Elgar home. When friends dropped in for the evening, they brought their instruments so they could play chamber music. Edward always begged to stay up and listen. When he was a little older, he went to the church to listen to his father practice the organ. Edward also spent as much time as he could in his father's music shop because he enjoyed trying to play the different instruments there.

Mr. Elgar soon realized that his son had musical talent; and when Edward was seven, he was sent to a school in Worcester known as The Ladies School. It was in this school that Edward was given his first piano lessons. Somehow he did not enjoy studying the piano; he had already made up his mind that he wanted to become a violinist.

Mr. Elgar agreed to let his son study the violin. The boy had his first lessons with Mr. Frederic Spray, a violinist of the Worcester Glee Club Orchestra. Edward advanced so rapidly that he was soon playing in the orchestra with his teacher.

When Edward was eleven years old, he was sent to a school called Littleon House. This was a small school of about twenty-five or thirty boys. The headmaster was a Mr. Francis Reeves. On Edward's first day of school, Master Reeves asked for Edward's name, and the boy replied, "Edward Elgar." Master Reeves thought the answer was not a polite one, and he said rather angrily, "Say, *sir*." Edward was a little confused, and he quickly said, "Sir Edward Elgar." Of course this was not what Master Reeves had meant, and Edward did not dream at that time that some day he would be "Sir Edward Elgar."

Edward worked very hard at school, and he also studied many musical subjects by himself. He read books on counterpoint and on orchestration, found in the warehouse of his father's music shop. While the other boys in the school were playing cricket, an English game played with balls and bats, Edward was doing his counterpoint exercises.

When Edward was fifteen years old he had to leave school. The Elgar family was a large one, and it was necessary for Edward to earn some money. Edward became an apprentice in a law office in Worcester. He was unhappy doing this sort of work. The only thing he really wanted to do was to become a musician. Mr. Elgar was understanding, and Edward was permitted to leave the law office and to study music seriously.

Edward began to practice the violin more than ever. In order to earn some money, he gave violin lessons, he helped his father in the music shop, and he became assistant organist to his father at St. George's Church. Besides all this, he had taught himself to play the bassoon; and he and his brother Frank, who played the oboe, gave little concerts together.

The next position Edward held was a rather important one. Besides being accompanist for the Worcester Glee Club, he also arranged and composed music for them. At the same time he continued his work as violinist in the orchestra of the Worcester Choral Society. He still had not given up hope of becoming a concert violinist.

When Edward reached the age of twenty, he had saved up a little money and was able to go to London to take some violin lessons with the well-known teacher, Adolph Pollitzer.

After the first lesson Mr. Pollitzer gave Edward a difficult exercise book and suggested that Edward prepare a few of them for his next lesson. When Edward came for his second lesson, Mr. Pollitzer asked him which exercises he had prepared. Edward modestly said, "the whole book."

Mr. Pollitzer was very much impressed with Edward's ability, but unfortunately Edward had to return to Worcester very soon. He had only saved up enough money for five lessons.

Back home again, Edward, inspired by Mr. Pollitzer's ideas, continued working on the violin. He also began to compose a symphony. He used the beautiful Mozart G minor Symphony as a model. Edward always said that he never did anything in his whole musical life that was more valuable to him than this. It is amazing how much Edward was able to accomplish by himself. He was later called the "self-taught musician."

In the year 1879 Edward was made conductor of the Worcester Glee Club, and he also became the bandmaster at the County Lunatic Asylum. This last position was not quite as strange as it sounds. Edward went to the asylum one day a week and conducted a band made up of the attendants at the hospital. He also taught the men to play instruments such as the flute, oboe, clarinet, double bass, piano, violin, and bombardon (a kind of tuba). Edward even composed music for the band; one of his compositions was called *Quadrilles for an Eccentric Orchestra.*

Each year Edward's work seemed to increase. When he was twenty-four years old, he was chosen to be the first violinist in an orchestra in Birmingham. This orchestra was a much more important one than the one in Worcester. In spite of the increased work, Edward still had time for composing. He was an ambitious young man and accomplished a great deal.

One of Elgar's early compositions was music for a children's play called *The Wand of Youth.* The performance of the music for the play became quite a family affair. Mr. Elgar and an uncle played the violins, Frank played the bassoon. When, at the last minute, it was discovered that a double bass was needed and none could be found, Edward and his brother made a double bass. They broke up a packing case, which they found in their father's music shop, and with the help of many nails and a set of strings built the instrument. Edward quickly taught his sister Lucy how to play it, and the performance was a great success.

For a long time Edward had wanted to go to Leipzig, Germany, because Leipzig was then the great musical center of Europe. At the end of 1882, when he was twenty-five years old, he had saved up enough money to realize his ambition for a few weeks. Edward heard much music in Leipzig, and he came back to Worcester determined to become an important composer.

It was after his return to Worcester that he had his first real encouragement as a composer. His composition *Serenade Mauresque* was performed by the Birmingham Symphony, and another composition, *Sevillana,* was played by the Crystal Palace Orchestra in London.

Edward decided now that he must have more time to spend composing, and he gave up a few of his many jobs. However, he did have to earn money, so he continued his organ playing at St. George's Church, he kept his job as the conductor of the Worcester Philharmonic Orchestra, and he also gave violin lessons.

One of Edward's new violin pupils was Miss Caroline Alice Robert. She was not only a good violin pupil but also became a great friend and admirer of her professor. Friendship turned to love, and Caroline and Edward were married on May 8, 1889. Mrs. Elgar encouraged and helped her husband to become a really important composer. They had one daughter, Carice, whom Elgar loved very much.

For Carice, Elgar composed a little piano piece called *Salut d'Amour.* This piece has become one of Elgar's most popular compositions. Besides an arrangement that Elgar made for small orchestra, it has been arranged for twenty-two different instruments.

Finally, even Elgar's own city of Worcester began to recognize him as a promising composer. He was invited to compose an overture for the big annual concert of the Worcester Festival. In this composition, his *Froissart Overture,* Elgar began to explore new ways of writing for the different instruments in the orchestra. He wanted to use each instrument in such a way that its music would blend with the other instruments and still retain its own peculiar qualities.

Elgar's next important compositions were *The Black Knight* for chorus and orchestra, the clever orchestra piece *Enigma Variations,* and the important oratorio

The Dream of Gerontius. It was with *The Dream of Gerontius* that Elgar revolutionized the form of the oratorio. Up until that time the famous oratorios, like Handel's *Messiah* and Mendelssohn's *Elijah,* had been written in such a way that some parts of the work were more important than other parts, and the various choruses and arias stood apart from each other. Elgar's *Dream of Gerontius* was written so that each part flowed into the next and every part was equally important.

When this oratorio had its first performance in Birmingham, England, it was not successful. People could not understand this new way of writing an oratorio. However, when it was performed in Düsseldorf, Germany, the following year, the important composer Richard Strauss made a speech about the work and called Elgar "the most progressive English musician." With this, Elgar was on his way to becoming well-known all over the world.

Elgar composed a set of six marches known as the *Pomp and Circumstance Marches.* These became extremely popular. There is hardly a band in the world that has not played them at one time or another. The first one of the set is particularly well-known, and the Trio, or middle part of the march has had words put to it. It is known as *Land of Hope and Glory*. Here are a few bars of this music:

In England this is as popular as the national anthem, *God Save The King*.

When someone asked Elgar why a composer who had written such an important oratorio as *The Dream of Gerontius* also wrote marches, he said that he did not see why soldiers should march only to "poor stuff."

Elgar was asked to compose a *Coronation Ode* for the coronation of King Edward VII, which was to be held on June 14, 1902. He wrote the composition, but the coronation had to be postponed because the King suddenly had to have an appendicitis operation. When the work was performed at a concert in London on October 26, 1902, the applause was so loud that the audience had to be asked to stop clapping so that the concert could go on.

At about this time Elgar's mother died quite unexpectedly. Elgar had been much devoted to her. She had given him a great love of books. He could still remember listening to her read to him when he was a young boy. Many times he had not even understood all that she read, but he had enjoyed the sound and the rhythm of the words.

His next important work was his oratorio *The Apostoles*. The idea for this composition had come to Elgar many years before. One day at Littleton House, Master Reeves had told the class the story of the faith and courage of the twelve Apostles, and Elgar had never forgotten it. Perhaps his own courage and determination to become an important composer were inspired by this story.

By this time Elgar had received many honors. He had an honorary degree of Doctor of Music from Cambridge University; he had been knighted by the King; he had an honorary degree of Doctor of Music from Oxford University; he had been invited to come to the United States where he had been given the honorary degree of Doctor of Music from Yale University; and he had the "Order of Merit" given to him by the King. Sometimes the letters O. M. (Of Merit) are placed after Elgar's name. The most touching of all his honors was given to him by his home town. He was given "the keys to the city." His father, who was then very old and feeble, looked out of a window as the procession headed by Edward passed on its way to the Cathedral. The old musician had tears in his eyes as he waved to his son.

Even though Elgar was so busy with his musical activities, he always found time for his hobbies. He loved to romp with his dogs, he enjoyed a game of golf, and he was interested in doing experiments in chemistry. At one time Elgar had three dogs, a Scottie, Meg, a Cairn, Nina, and a black and white spaniel, Marco. He also liked to go to dog shows. Nothing would stop him from enjoying an event of this kind. Once, when he went with a friend, it had rained all of the night before and the place where the show was to be held was almost completely under water. In order to pass from one tent to another to see the dogs, Elgar and his friend had to paddle along on duck-boards.

Elgar spent many hours in his laboratory. He had built a little shed called The Ark near his home, and it was there that he did his experiments in chemistry. Once Elgar was fooling around with a few chemicals when a musical idea came to his mind. He left the mixture and forgetting all about his experiment went to his studio. All of a sudden there was a loud crash; the liquids had exploded! Fortunately, the only damage was a blown-up water barrel. A little while later when Elgar was taking a walk, a neighbor came up to him and said, "Sir Edward, did you hear that awful noise?"

Sir Edward pretended to know nothing about it.

For many years Elgar thought about composing a symphony, and finally in the summer of 1908 he wrote his Symphony Number One in A♭ Major. It had its first performance in Manchester, England, on December 3, 1908.

The following year Elgar composed a beautiful violin concerto. It was first performed by the Austrian violinist, Fritz Kreisler, on November 10, 1910. His next composition for orchestra, called *Falstaff,* was Elgar's favorite one. Elgar loved the plays of Shakespeare, and this piece is based on Shakespeare's character Falstaff.

In August, 1914, when Elgar and his wife were in Scotland on a holiday they heard of the outbreak of the First World War. They hurried home and until peace was declared, more than four years later, Elgar composed mostly patriotic music. Some of his compositions were *Carillon,* the set of songs called *Fringes of the Fleet,* and a work in three parts for chorus and orchestra called *The Spirit of England.*

During the summer of 1918, when there was the feeling that the war would soon end, Elgar went to the country. His mind was a little more at ease, and he worked on three different compositions at the same time, a violin sonata, a string quartet, and a 'cello concerto. The 'cello concerto was played for the first time by the English 'cellist, Felix Salmond, in London, on October 27, 1919.

The following spring, his devoted wife, Caroline, became ill and died quite suddenly. This was a great loss to Elgar, and he did not compose a note of music for several years. His first work when he returned to music was an arrangement of some of Bach's works for orchestra. Elgar was always a great lover of Bach's music and he often said that hardly a day went by that he did not play some of the wonderful preludes and fugues from the *Well Tempered Clavichord.*

In 1924 Elgar was appointed Master of the King's Music. Elgar's duties were to compose music for the King, to attend concerts with the King and Queen, and to take care of the Royal collection of instruments. Elgar did not live in the palace, but he lived in an apartment close by.

Sir Edward Elgar had become the greatest and best loved English composer since Henry Purcell, who lived in the seventeenth century.

To give a special honor to Sir Edward on his seventy-fifth birthday, the British Broadcasting Company made a festival of three concerts of his music. At the festivities it was also announced that Sir Edward had been invited to compose a new symphony, his third, especially for the BBC.

Sir Edward was very happy about this, but he never finished the symphony. He became seriously ill, and after a few months he died in Worcester on February 23, 1934.

Among Elgar's compositions are the *Enigma Variations, Pomp and Circumstance Marches,* two symphonies, *The Dream of Gerontius, The Apostles,* violin concertos, 'cello concertos, piano pieces, songs, and orchestral compositions.

Besides introducing a new way of writing an oratorio, Elgar had a most unusual way of writing for an orchestra. No other composer had used the full sound of the orchestra so continuously without having the instruments ever sound crowded together. Elgar knew the special secret of each instrument.

In May, 1935, the cottage in Broadheath where Edward Elgar was born was bought by a group of men known as the Worcester Corporation. This has become an Elgar Museum, and in it are many of the composer's personal possessions.

Sergei Vassilievitch Rachmaninoff

1873—1943

Sergei Vassilievitch Rachmaninoff, usually just called Sergei Rachmaninoff, was born on April 2, 1873, in the lovely country village of Novgorod. At that time the Rachmaninoff family was living on their beautiful estate Onneg, situated in the northern part of Russia near the picturesque river Volchov.

Sergei's father, Vassili, was a handsome officer in the Russian Army. He was a rather musical man. However, it was Sergei's grandfather, Arkadi, who was the real musician in the family. He was an excellent pianist, and even when he was an old man, he practiced the piano for four hours every day.

Sergei's mother played the piano well enough to give her son his first lessons. On one occasion, when his Grandfather was coming for a visit, Sergei's mother taught him a few special pieces so that he could play a little concert.

The day arrived, and Sergei was very excited. His mother had dressed him in a new navy blue suit with a white collar, and his grandfather was waiting for him to come into the music room to perform. Just as Sergei was about to enter the room, his mother stopped him, examined his hands, and said, "I must cut your nails so you may play better." Sergei was so sure of himself that he exclaimed, "I'll play well anyhow, you have been teaching me for months!" At the time, Sergei was only four years old.

The elder Mr. Rachmaninoff was very much impressed with the talent that Sergei showed, and that evening he had a long talk with his son and daughter-in-law about the boy.

Sergei's father did not want him to become a musician. He had made plans to send Sergei to a military academy. However, Sergei's mother, who already had dreams of her son becoming a concert pianist, convinced her husband that his father was right. The boy must be trained to become a musician.

A young pianist, Anna Ornazkaya, who had just finished her studies at the St. Petersburg Conservatory, came to live with the Rachmaninoffs. She taught Sergei the piano, and in a few years he learned to play extremely well.

When Sergei was nine years old, Mademoiselle Ornazkaya thought that he played well enough to go to the Conservatory in St. Petersburg. Sergei looked forward to this because he had been told that St. Petersburg was a wonderful city with beautiful schools and churches and that the Conservatory was a fine school.

Unfortunately, things were not going very well at home. Mr. Rachmaninoff knew a great deal about the army, but he did not know very much about the business of managing an estate. Because of this the family lost almost all of their money, and beautiful Onneg was sold at an auction.

Grandmother Boutakova, Madame Rachmaninoff's mother, lived in St. Petersburg, and the family decided to go and live with her. In this way Sergei was able to become a student at the St. Petersburg Conservatory.

At first Sergei did very well at the Conservatory, but then, probably because he was ahead of the class, he became lazy and bored. Sometimes he did not even go to his classes, but went ice skating instead. Another favorite game was hopping on the back of a horse-drawn streetcar in order to get a free ride. One day his sister Helena saw him doing this; she was very much upset. She made Sergei promise that he would never do this again.

Helena was five years older than Sergei and a remarkable girl. She had a beautiful voice and a fine mind. It was she who made Sergei realize that he must do his lessons if he was going to accomplish anything. Helena introduced Sergei to the songs of Tchaikowsky, and his favorite became *None But the Lonely Heart*. Helena sang it over and over again to please her young brother. Helena had dreams of becoming an opera star, and Sergei now wanted to become a great composer like Tchaikowsky.

Unfortunately Helena suddenly became quite ill before she reached her seventeenth birthday. No doctor could help her, and she died within a short time. At first the shock was such a great one that Sergei could not concentrate on any of his work. However, as soon as he felt a little better, he became one of the best students at the Conservatory. He did exceptionally well in piano, theory, and harmony. He was determined to carry out the plans that Helena had made for him. He was going to become an important musician!

Sergei adored his grandmother, and he used to love to go to church with her. Every Sunday as they walked home from church, Grandmother Boutakova would say, "If when we get home you will play for memory some of the songs you have heard this morning at St. Isaac's Cathedral, I will give you twenty-five kopecs" (about twenty-five cents). Sergei was able to play whatever he had heard; and in order to keep up his interest, his grandmother raised her reward every Sunday. Finally Sergei laughed and said, "Soon you will go bankrupt on account of me."

Although Sergei was progressing very well in his lessons, his mother felt that he needed a change. Just at that time Sergei's cousin Alexander Siloti, who was a concert pianist, was in St. Petersburg, and Madame Rachmaninoff spoke to him about Sergei. Siloti said that the only teacher for Sergei was his former teacher, Nikolai Sverev. Sverev lived in Moscow and taught at the Moscow Conservatory. It was decided that after the summer was over Sergei would go to Moscow.

That summer was a happy one for Sergei because he went to his grandmother's country home, Bovrissovo. He swam and fished and took long walks in the woods with the neighborhood boys. He also practiced the piano and gave little concerts for his grandmother.

However, the summer soon came to an end, and it

was time for him to leave for Moscow. His grandmother took him to the train, and tied a little bag filled with roubles, which are Russian dollars, around his neck. When she kissed him goodby, Sergei said, "Some day you will be proud of me."

It was a rainy August morning in 1885 when Sergei arrived in Moscow. He spent the first three days with his aunt, Madame Siloti. This was a good thing because it helped him get over his loneliness. Then he went to live in the home of his teacher, Sverev. There were two other boys living in Sverev's home, and the three "cubs," as they were called, became great friends. Sverev's sister took care of the boys and disciplined them a great deal. This was especially good for Sergei. In a short time Sergei changed from a lazy, mischievous boy to a quiet, serious student. Sverev was especially proud of Sergei and asked him to play for many visitors. Sergei also did well in his counterpoint and harmony studies.

When Sergei was thirteen years old, he arranged a symphony of Tchaikowsky's for two pianos. In order to do this, he had to teach himself how to read all the parts that Tchaikowsky had written for the different instruments of the orchestra. This is called reading a musical score. Sergei's arrangement of the symphony was such a good one that one day when Tchaikowsky came to visit Sverev, Sverev showed it to Tchaikowsky. Sverev also had Sergei play the piano for Tchaikowsky, who became most enthusiastic about the young pianist. At that time Tchaikowsky was a teacher in composition at the Moscow Conservatory, and he took a great interest in Sergei.

After Sergei had taken his last harmony examination of the year, he received the highest mark that was given, a 5+. Tchaikowsky was so pleased when he heard about this, that he himself examined Sergei's paper. He made the mark even higher by adding three more plus signs. Now it looked like this—

+
+5+!
+

Sergei was excited because Tchaikowsky was his idol. To please the great master even more, Sergei had made up his mind to graduate from the Conservatory with the highest honor that was given, The Great Gold Medal. In order to compete for this honor, Sergei had to accomplish three things. First, he had to write a fugue, second he had to perform certain piano pieces, and third, he had to write a one act opera in a month's time. Sergei passed the first two parts with flying colors, but it was the third part that really surprised everyone. After two week's time, the director of the Conservatory asked to see how much of the opera Sergei had completed. Not only was Sergei's opera finished, but he had taken his last few roubles and had had the score bound in leather with the title of the opera, *Aleko,* engraved in gold letters on top of the score.

Sergei's wish came true, and he was awarded The Great Gold Medal. His name was added to the Roll of Honor, and it was also inscribed on the marble tablet which hung in the vestibule of the Conservatory.

Soon Sergei's accomplishment was known all over Moscow. An important publisher, Mr. Gutheil, offered to publish the opera, and *Aleko* had its first performance in the Bolshoi Theatre in Moscow in the spring of 1893. A large audience was present at the performance. After it was over, there were shouts of "Composer! Composer!" Sergei bowed again and again. It was a thrilling experience for a young man of twenty. But what pleased Sergei most of all was that his idol, Tchaikowsky, was in the audience.

After the great success of *Aleko,* Sergei worked harder than ever on his compositions. Also in 1893 some of his piano pieces were published. Among them was the Prelude in C♯ Minor which was to become his most popular work. This piece is often called by its nickname *The Bells of Moscow*. It is played by students and concert performers all over the world.

Here are a few measures of the Prelude.

Sergei's next compositions were a piece for orchestra called *The Rock*, a *Fantasia* for two pianos, and his Symphony Number One in D minor. The symphony was not a success, and Sergei became very unhappy. Not only did he lose confidence in himself, but he became ill. It was only with the help of a Dr. Dahl, and with the encouragement of his cousin Natalie Satin, that he gradually became himself again.

After Sergei recovered, he was invited to be one of the conductors of a new opera company, The Mamontov Opera Company. This work helped him meet many important singers. Among them was Feodor Challiapin who became one of the world's greatest basses. Challiapin sang Sergei's songs at his concerts. One song, *Fate,* became particularly well known because of him. Rachmaninoff was inspired by Beethoven's *Fate Symphony* when he composed this song.

About this time Rachmaninoff's cousin Siloti, played the C♯ Minor Prelude at a concert in London, and it became successful immediately. Copies of the piece were sold by the thousands all over Europe and even in the United States.

Fortunately for Rachmaninoff, his cousin Siloti was a generous man. He gave young Rachmaninoff enough money so that for two years he did not have to do anything but compose.

Rachmaninoff worked hard, and during this time he composed more piano preludes, a cantata called *Spring*, a 'cello sonata, and many songs.

Almost at the same time, Rachmaninoff's friendship with his cousin Natalie Satin became a serious one. They were married on April 29, 1902. She was a wonderful woman, and their marriage was a happy one.

Soon after their marriage, the Rachmaninoffs settled in Moscow. There Rachmaninoff practiced the piano and composed new works. He had just finished his second Piano Concerto in C Minor, and when he played it in Moscow for the first time, it was a great success. Its beautiful melodies were as moving at that time as they are now.

Here are a few measures of the melody of the third movement of this concerto:

In the next few years Rachmaninoff worked hard conducting operas at the Bolshoi Theatre in Moscow. Two of his own operas, *The Miserly Knight* and *Francesca da Rimini,* were also performed and were extremely successful.

At the end of a day's work, Rachmaninoff's greatest joy was to go home and play with his first daughter, Irene; but sometimes he was so tired that even this was an effort. Mrs. Rachmaninoff noticed that her husband was not looking very well and encouraged him to take a vacation. The family went off to Dresden, Germany.

In Dresden, Rachmaninoff felt much better, and the quiet atmosphere was good for practicing and composing. While they were there, the Rachmaninoff's second daughter, Tatiana, was born, on June 21, 1907.

During the time that Rachmaninoff was in Dresden, he received an invitation to come to the United States and give some concerts. He was happy about this, and the family went back to Moscow immediately.

In order to have the peace and quiet necessary to prepare for these concerts and also to compose a new piano concerto, (his third, "especially for America") Rachmaninoff and his family went to their country estate in the suburbs of Moscow.

Rachmaninoff was fond of the country, and he especially loved to ride and train the horses that were on the estate. He rode as well as any American cowboy. Another hobby was driving the latest model automobile. In those days the horse was faster than the auto, but Rachmaninoff drove his car all over the countryside. People were always amused at the sight of Rachmaninoff at the wheel of his car dressed up in a long white linen coat with a special cap on his head and big goggles on his eyes.

After the summer was over, the family returned to Moscow; and in the autumn of that year (1909) Rachmaninoff left for the United States. The trip without his family was a lonely one for the composer. However, when he finally arrived in the United States and was met by some friendly American musicians, he was a little more cheerful.

Rachmaninoff's beautiful piano playing and his new Third Piano Concerto were very successful. Rachmaninoff was invited to play in other cities besides New York, and wherever he went, the audiences were enthusiastic.

Rachmaninoff fell in love with the United States; and when he left for Moscow three months later, he knew that someday he would return.

Between the years 1910 and 1914 Rachmaninoff was extremely busy. He was Vice-President of the Imperial Russian Musical Society, and he was also the conductor of the Moscow Philharmonic Symphony Orchestra. He was only able to take the time for a few concert tours in Germany and England.

In 1914, Rachmaninoff finally decided that the time had come for a vacation. He and his family went to Italy. In Italy he composed a piece for orchestra called *The Bells.* This piece was inspired by a poem called "The Bells," written by the American poet Edgar Allen Poe. Rachmaninoff had always enjoyed anything about bells. Perhaps he was reminded of his childhood days when he listened to the vesper bells of the churches in Novgorod.

During the Italian visit, the Rachmaninoff children became ill and the family hurried back to Moscow. No sooner had they settled in their country home and nursed the children back to health, than they heard that war had begun. The next years were sad ones. All of Rachmaninoff's concerts were cancelled. The only playing Rachmaninoff did was for charity and for the wounded soldiers. He composed only one important work during all the war years; that was *Vesper Mass* for a chorus of boys and men.

The war changed many things in Russia. After the Russian Revolution of 1917, the government became one that was ruled by the peasants instead of by the aristocrats, or White Russians as they were called. Many of the White Russians left Russia at this time because they would not accept the new government. Rachmaninoff and his family were among them. They went to Stockholm, Sweden, arriving there during the Christmas season of 1917.

That Christmas was not a very joyous one for the Rachmaninoffs. They were without a home, and most of their possessions had been left in Russia. Rachmaninoff gave some concerts in Sweden, but he was not really happy until he was again asked to come to the United States. This time the entire family went together.

It was on the first Armistice Day of 1918 that the Rachmaninoff family arrived in New York. There was great joy in the hearts of all the people that day, and Rachmaninoff felt that his family, too, would be happy in their new, adopted home.

Although Rachmaninoff had not been in New York for nine years, he was not forgotten. Everywhere he went he heard his Prelude in C♯ Minor!

Rachmaninoff played many, many concerts during his thirty years in the United States, and people always found it a thrilling experience to attend one. Whether Rachmaninoff played his own compositions or those of other composers, his playing was beautiful and exciting. Sometimes he conducted the orchestra and played one of his own concertos at the same time. When he finished, the applause of the large audience sounded like claps of thunder.

Eventually a time came when Rachmaninoff's health began to fail, and, at the doctor's suggestion, the family moved from New York to Beverly Hills, California. The climate in California helped him a little, but Rachmaninoff insisted on giving concerts and the strain was too much for a man of almost seventy years.

During a concert in New Orleans, Rachmaninoff became very ill. He was rushed back to California, but nothing could be done for him. He died on March 28, 1943, in his home in Beverly Hills.

Rachmaninoff was a great pianist and a fine composer. Among Rachmaninoff's compositions are: the four piano concertos, the *Rhapsody on a Theme by Paganini* for piano and orchestra, preludes and other pieces for the piano, symphonies, operas, and songs. Of all of Rachmaninoff's compositions, it is his piano music that is most distinguished. The beautiful melodies of these pieces will never be forgotten!

Aaron Copland

1900—

In the year 1875 Aaron Copland's father, then a young man of fifteen, left his native Russia for England. When he arrived in England, an incident happened which permanently changed his last name. The immigration officer misunderstood the spelling of his name and wrote down "Harris Copland" instead of "Harris Caplan."

Harris Copland spent two years in England and then decided to go to the United States. He settled in Brooklyn, New York, and became a merchant. In a few years he had saved up enough money to buy a small department store. The business prospered; and when Harris Copland was twenty-five years old, he married a young lady named Sarah Mittenthal. She, too, had originally come from Russia. Harris Copland was not at all musical, but his wife, Sarah, sang and played the piano a little.

The Coplands had five children. Aaron, who was the youngest one in the family, was born in Brooklyn on November 14, 1900.

Aaron's two sisters and two brothers all had music lessons, but nothing much was accomplished. When the time came for Aaron to have lessons, his parents felt that they had already "wasted enough money on music lessons." As it turned out, Aaron was the only one who was talented; and he begged for music lessons. One day his older sister, Laurine, said "Come on, Aaron, sit down, and I will show you how to play the piano." After six months of lessons, Aaron had progressed so rapidly that Laurine had to give up. She patted her young brother on the shoulder and said, "You know more than I learned in eight years of study, and I can't teach you anything else."

Aaron was eleven and a half years old at that time, and for the next year and a half he practiced by himself. When he reached the age of thirteen, he decided that he must have regular piano lessons. He finally convinced his mother of his need, and Mrs. Copland said, "All right, if you want to find the teacher yourself, we don't have any objection to your studying."

Aaron had heard of a Mr. Leopold Wolfsohn, who had a piano studio in Brooklyn. One day Aaron plucked up enough courage to knock on Mr. Wolfsohn's door and ask him for lessons. Mr. Wolfsohn was happy to accept such an eager student, and Aaron became one of his best pupils.

Another of Aaron's ambitions was to become a composer. When he was only eight and a half years old, he composed a song for his sister-in-law, Dorothy.

Aaron had been ill, and the song was his way of thanking Dorothy for some cherries that she brought him. When Aaron was about thirteen years old, he decided to compose an opera. Laurine had gone to see a performance of the opera *Cavalleria Rusticana.* The Italian composer, Mascagni, had written the music for this opera, but Aaron decided that he was going to write his own music for the words. He did not get very far because he soon realized that before he could compose well, he had to know something about harmony. Harmony is the study of chords and how to use them in writing music. Aaron discussed this problem with his piano teacher, and later Mr. Wolfsohn helped Aaron find a harmony teacher.

In the fall of 1917 Aaron began weekly harmony and composition lessons with Mr. Rubin Goldmark. At their first meeting, Mr. Goldmark looked at Aaron and said, "What do you want to become a composer for!" This was a real challenge to the ambitious boy.

That year Aaron worked very hard on piano, harmony, composition, and his studies at school. The following year, 1918, Aaron graduated from Boy's High School in Brooklyn, and then he definitely decided to make music his life's work.

Although Mr. Goldmark was a fine teacher, there was one thing about his teaching that made Aaron unhappy. His ideas were old-fashioned. Aaron liked to experiment with new chords and new rhythms, and when he did this Mr. Goldmark called him a "musical rebel."

One day Aaron brought a piano piece that he had just composed, called *The Cat and The Mouse,* to Mr. Goldmark. Mr. Goldmark looked at it, threw it aside, and said, "How do you expect me to criticize such music?" From that time on Aaron carried on his experiments by himself; and to please Mr. Goldmark, he wrote compositions following all the rules.

Aaron studied with Mr. Goldmark for three years. During this time he wrote works which he called his *Juvenilia* (youthful works). He composed violin pieces, piano pieces, pieces for the 'cello, and a piano sonata. Aaron also included *The Cat and The Mouse* and a song called *Old Poem* in his list of juvenilia.

At the same time Aaron studied composition with Mr. Goldmark, he also continued his piano lessons with Mr. Wolfsohn. He later studied the piano with Mr. Victor Wittgenstein and Mr. Clarence Adler.

In the 1920's it was considered necessary for a young American composer to finish his studies in Europe. Since Paris was then the center of music, Aaron had dreams of going to Paris.

One day when he was reading a magazine called *Musical America,* he noticed an advertisement for a music school for Americans that was going to open during the summer of 1921. The school was to be held in the beautiful Palace of Fontainebleau in Paris. Aaron was so enthusiastic about this news that he was the first one to answer the advertisement. His name was put at the head of the list.

Aaron discussed the idea with his parents, who were not too anxious for him to become a composer. It was decided, however, that he would be given the opportunity to go to Fontainebleau. Aaron proudly told his parents that he had saved up some money and that he would contribute it towards his trip. For several summers Aaron had worked in his father's store, he had had some other odd jobs, and each week he had even put away some of his allowance. He had had hopes of going to Paris someday, and now his dreams would come true.

Aaron sailed for France on June 9, 1921. On the ship he found other students who were also going to Fontainebleau. This was a lucky thing for Aaron because his early student days had been spent by himself, and he had missed the companionship of other music students.

The trip was a good one, and when the students arrived in Fontainebleau, they found the palace and the surrounding grounds very beautiful. The girls lived at the palace, and the boys lived nearby. However, all the students met for their meals, which were served in a dining room of the palace.

The classes at Fontainebleau began on June 24. Aaron was happy with everything about the school except his composition teacher, Paul Vidal. He turned out to be as old-fashioned in his teaching as Mr. Goldmark had been.

One day Aaron was discussing his problem with another student. She told him about a wonderful teacher in the school named Nadia Boulanger. At first Aaron was not enthusiastic about this. "No one to my knowledge has ever thought of studying composition with a woman," he said. "Everyone knows that the world has never produced a first-rate woman composer, so it follows that no woman could possibly hope to teach composition." Finally, however, Aaron consented to go and listen to one of Nadia Boulanger's classes. He was absolutely amazed at her method of teaching, and he began to study with her immediately. His ideas about "a woman composition teacher" soon changed. Aaron became one of Nadia Boulanger's most enthusiastic pupils.

With financial help from home, Aaron was able to remain in Paris and study with Mlle. Boulanger for three years. Aaron later said that being a pupil of this remarkable woman was the most important musical event of his whole life.

While Aaron was a student in Paris, several of his compositions were published. The first one was the piano piece *The Cat and The Mouse,* and Aaron was proud to receive five hundred francs (about $35) for it.

During these three years Aaron also heard much new music or Modern Music, as it is called. In modern music composers experiment with new chords, new scales, and new rhythms. Among the composers whose works Aaron heard for the first time were Schoenberg, Stravinsky, and Bartok.

Many of these new works were given their first performances at the Concerts Koussevitzky. Serge Koussevitzky was then a young Russian conductor who organized these concerts especially to give young composers an opportunity to have their works performed. Mr. Koussevitzky later came to the United States and became the conductor of the Boston Symphony Orchestra. He always helped young composers, and Aaron became one of his favorites. Koussevitzky once jokingly said "A balanced symphonic diet must include Vitamin C: C-ontemporary Music (modern music).

During Aaron's student years in Paris he composed a *Passacaglia* for piano, a song for soprano with the accompaniment of flute and clarinet, a *Rondino* for string quartet, and most important of all, a one act ballet called *Grohg*. This was Aaron's first piece for orchestra, and in it he experimented with many different rhythms. It was also Aaron's first ballet, and he later became the most important American composer for the ballet.

At the end of Aaron's third year in Paris, it was necessary for him to go back to the United States. Before he left Paris, in June of 1924, Mlle. Boulanger, told him that she was coming to the United States the following year to give some concerts. She asked Aaron to compose an organ piece for her to play with the orchestras in New York and Boston. Aaron sailed for home happy and excited. This was the greatest honor that Mlle. Boulanger could have given him.

That summer Aaron had to earn some money, and he got a position as the pianist of a trio in a summer hotel in Milford, Pennsylvania. Whenever he had time, he worked on his organ piece, which was called an *Organ Symphony*. However, Aaron did not finish the piece until he returned to New York the following fall.

The first performance of the *Organ Symphony* was given in the fall of 1924 in New York, with Dr. Damrosch conducting the orchestra and Mlle. Boulanger playing the organ. An unexpected incident occurred at the performance. When the piece was finished, Dr. Damrosch turned around and said to the audience, "If a young man at the age of twenty-three can write a symphony like that, in five years he will be able to commit murder." This piece was just "too modern" for Dr. Damrosch. "Fortunately," said Aaron, "his prophecy came to nothing."

However, Mr. Koussevitzky heard the symphony and was enthusiastic about it. He asked Mr. Copland to compose a special piece for a concert of all modern music which was going to be given the following winter in New York City.

Just at that time, in 1925, Copland was chosen to receive a sum of money from the Guggenheim Memorial Foundation. He was given $2,500 a year for two years. This made it possible for him to spend all his time on composition.

Copland worked hard on the special piece for Mr. Koussevitzky. In this composition, which was called *Music for the Theatre,* Copland used jazz. This was the first time that jazz had been used in a symphonic composition. Copland wanted this piece to sound very American, and jazz had grown out of African-American folk music.

Mr. Koussevitzky was so impressed with *Music for the Theatre,* that he asked Copland to compose another piece for him. Copland did, and in this composition, called *Concerto for Piano and Orchestra,* he again used jazz.

When Copland played the *Concerto for Piano and Orchestra* for the first time with the Boston Symphony Orchestra, it was not liked. One critic, writing about the piece in the newspaper, called it "that terrible concerto," and he also called Mr. Copland "The Ogre." It takes time for a new idea to catch on because when the concerto was performed in New York fifteen years later, a critic wrote that Mr. Copland's concerto was the best piece either by an American or a European composer that used symphonic jazz.

After *Music for The Theatre* and *Concerto for Piano and Orchestra,* Copland did not experiment with jazz anymore. However, he did use other folk music in his compositions. Sometimes he used the tunes just as he found them, and other times he changed them to fit his own ideas.

Copland loved Mexico and the music of Mexico. He made several trips to that country and one of his compositions *El Salon Mexico* is based on Mexican folk themes. The music is tuneful and rhythmic, and the piece is even named after a popular dance hall in Mexico City, "Salon Mexico."

When *El Salon Mexico* was first played in London in 1938, it was so well liked that in some ways it was really a turning point for Copland. It was after this performance that the English publishers, Boosey and Hawkes, gave him a long term contract. They promised to publish each new work as soon as it was composed.

Most important of Mr. Copland's contributions to modern American music are his ballets. Among them are *Hear Ye! Hear Ye!, Billy the Kid, Rodeo* and *Appalachian Spring. Billy the Kid* is particularly popular. It is a ballet about a Western badman. In it Copland uses some cowboy songs.

Here are a few measures of the music:

During the Second World War, Copland wrote several patriotic compositions, and one of them, *A Lincoln Portrait,* is performed often. In this piece Mr. Copland has a narrator recite some of Abraham Lincoln's great speeches to the accompaniment of the music.

Copland has also written music especially for school children. No other important composer has ever done this. One of these works is a play opera called *The Second Hurricane*. This composition was performed for the first time on April 21, 1937, at the Henry Street Music School in New York City. The children themselves managed the whole performance. Some of them sang and acted, some of them played in the orchestra, and others built the scenery

Here are a few measures of this music:

Another piece, especially for a high school orchestra, is called *Outdoor Overture*. And two of his short piano pieces were written for piano students. They are called *Sunday Afternoon Music* and *Young Pioneers*. In *Young Pioneers* Mr. Copland does not refer to our early American ancestors, but to the young people who are pioneers brave enough to adventure into the mysteries of the new harmonies and rhythms of twentieth century music.

Mr. Copland feels that some music in any period must be written because it is needed for that period. Bach composed music for the church, Haydn and Mozart wrote light music to amuse their royal patrons. Today there is need for school music, music for radio audiences, music for television, music for records, and music for the movies. Mr. Copland has composed music for every one of these.

Several of his movie scores have been unusually successful. Among them are *Our Town, Of Mice and Men, The North Star, The Red Pony* and *The Heiress*. The music for *The Heiress* won an Academy Award for the best movie score of 1950.

Besides all the different kinds of music that Mr. Copland has composed, he has written four books on music: *What to Listen for in Music, Our New Music, Music and Imagination,* and *Copland on Music.*

For the past twenty-two years Mr. Copland has been head of the composition department at Tanglewood, a summer school in Lenox, Massachusetts. Not only have his classes been an inspiration to many young composers, but he has also given lectures on modern music, which have been one of the most important events of the school.

Mr. Copland has introduced much of our modern American music to audiences in the United States, as well as in the Latin American countries. His own compositions have been chosen to represent the United States at music festivals all over the world.

Among Mr. Copland's compositions are: three symphonies, many other orchestral works, piano compositions, songs, an opera called *The Tender Land,* chamber music works, and ballets. One of Mr. Copland's latest compositions is called *Orchestral Connotations.* This work was especially written for the opening of Lincoln Center, a new center for the performing arts in New York City. The piece had its first performance on September 23, 1962, by the New York Philharmonic Orchestra with Leonard Bernstein conducting.

In recent years Mr. Copland has added another accomplishment to his list: He has conducted orchestras in England, France, Japan, and the Soviet Union. In 1960, when the Boston Symphony Orchestra played concerts in the Far East, Copland was the guest conductor.

Mr. Copland has received honorary degrees from

many colleges and universities in the United States for his outstanding accomplishments in music. There is no doubt that Mr. Copland has been one of the greatest influences in America in recent years.

Glossary

Accompaniment—Any part of a piece of music which supports the melody. Also the part played by an orchestra or a piano with the soloist.

Adagio—A slow, leisurely tempo. Also, music played at a slow tempo.

Air—A term for a song.

In the eighteenth century composers often called the slow movement of a dance suite an *air*.

Allegro—A fast, lively tempo. Also, music that is played at a fast tempo.

Anthem—A composition for voices usually with a religious text and performed in church.

A *National Anthem* is the official patriotic song of a country.

Aria—A song or a melody sung by one person with an accompaniment. It gives the singer a chance to "show off" his voice.

Arias are found in operas, cantatas, and oratorios.

Arrangement—A composition rewritten for an instrument or instruments that it was not written for at first, which changes the original piece.

Bagatelle—A "trifle" or a short piece of music usually for the piano.

Ballet—A story told by dancing and set to orchestral music.

Cantata—A composition for chorus and soloists in several movements that includes arias, duets, trios, etc. and chorales. It is usually accompanied by instruments.

Capellmeister—A German word for a musical director or for one who is in charge of music in a choir or an orchestra.

Celesta—An instrument that looks like a small piano. When it is played, a set of hammers strike against a set of metal bars, making a bell-like sound.

Chamber Music—Music written to be played in a room or a small hall. It is usually performed by trios, quartets or small combinations of players.

Chord—Two or more musical notes sounded together.

Clavichord—A keyboard instrument invented before the piano. In the piano the tone is made by felt hammers hitting the strings, but in the clavichord it is made by small metal wedges pressing on the strings. The sound that comes out is more delicate than that of the piano.

Concerto—A composition usually in three movements for a solo instrument with an orchestral accompaniment. (There are also concertos for two or three solo instruments)
Sometimes, as in Bach or Handel, a whole group of instruments are treated in a solo fashion. For instance, the Bach *Brandenburg Concertos*.

Counterpoint—The art of combining two or more melodies in such a way that although they are played together each one can be heard separately.

Court Musician—A musician who was employed by a king or a nobleman.

Development—The changing and elaborating of a musical theme by working in new harmonies and rhythms. The section of a work in which this is done.

Divertimento—A light composition of several short movements for a small group of instruments or an orchestra.
Often used as entertainment music in the eighteenth century.

Duet—Music for two voices or instruments with or without accompaniment. The music is divided as equally as possible.

Étude—Music to help improve the technique of the player, but written in an interesting way. Chopin's études for piano are among the most famous ones.

Folk Song—A song handed down from generation to generation which tells stories of the work and lives of simple people. The composer generally is not known.

Fugue—A composition in which there are several parts or voices. A fugue is built on a melody called a subject. First the subject is announced by itself and then it is imitated in the other voices, one after the other. Whenever a new voice plays the subject, the other voices play something else.

Harmony—The study of making chords and the way in which one chord is related to the other. A chord is built by using two, three, four or more notes which are sounded together.

Harpsichord—An instrument used before the invention of the piano, but later than the clavichord. Its shape resembles the shape of a grand piano, but it often has two keyboards. When a note is played on the harpsichord, the strings inside the instrument are plucked by a quill. This makes a lighter sound than the piano. The harpsichord is still used, especially to play music that was originally written for the instrument, like the Scarlatti sonatas.

Humoresque—A humorous or fanciful, often very light, composition.

Improvise—To make up music as one is singing or playing an instrument.

Invention—Short piece with one theme that is worked out in counterpoint. First the right hand plays the theme, then the left hand, and the hand that is waiting for its turn plays a counter theme. Johann Sebastian Bach composed the best known inventions.

Krakowiak—A Polish Dance in 2/4 time, popular in the nineteenth century. It was performed by a great many couples who shouted while they danced. The men also kicked their heels, which were covered with metal, and this made a loud noise.

Libretto—The story or words of an opera or a musical play.

Lieder—German word for songs; used mostly for the songs of Schubert, Schumann, and Brahms.

Mass—Composition for voices, usually accompanied by instruments, based on the ritual of the Roman Catholic Church.

Mazurka—A national Polish dance performed by four or eight couples. It is in 3/4 or 3/8 time and has a strong accent on the third, and sometimes the second beat of the measure.
Chopin wrote 52 mazurkas for the piano.

Minuet—A rather slow dance in 3/4 time. Very popular in the courts of Europe in the seventeenth and eighteenth centuries.
Sometimes a minuet is one movement of a sonata or a symphony.

Movement—A part, generally a separate and distinct part, of a longer musical composition. A symphony generally has four movements.

Opera—A story set to music for singers and orchestra. An opera is intended to be performed on a stage with scenery and costumes.

Opus—Usually abbreviated as "Op." Used with numbers to show the order of a composer's work. For instance: Op. 1 is a composer's first work.

Oratorio—A composition for vocal solos, chorus, and instrumental accompaniment. It generally tells a story, and is almost always based on a religious theme. An oratorio is sung without costumes, acting, or scenery.

Overture—Instrumental music played as an introduction to an opera or musical play. The overture usually includes melodies from the main songs which will follow. Sometimes it is a piece for orchestra that is not part of another work, like the *Academic Festival Overture* by Johannes Brahms.

Polka—A dance which originated in Bohemia, the old name for Czechoslovakia. The music is in 2/4 time and is played rather slowly, like a military march.
In the Czech language the world *polka* means half, and the main feature of the dance is its short half steps.

Polonaise—A dance which originated in Poland. It is written in 3/4 time and has a strong accent on the first beat. It is played in a stately way, almost like a march.

Chopin's polonaises are an expression of the heroism and patriotism of the Polish people.

Prelude—Short composition sometimes used to prepare a listener for other music which will follow. Other times preludes are separate little pieces in themselves, like Chopin's preludes for the piano (there are twenty-four of them).

Quartet—A composition for four instruments or voices.

Quodlibet—A humorous piece of music which includes snatches of well-known popular melodies. Several melodies are played together at the same time.

Requiem—A Mass sung in memory of someone who has died.

Rondo—A composition for either singers or instruments in which one main theme comes back again and again, even though other themes have been introduced.

Scherzo—A lively, humorous piece. In Italian, *scherzo* means joke.

Sonata—A composition for one or two instruments that usually has three or four movements.

Sonata Form—Form most often used in first movements of sonatas, symphonies and concertos.

The form is:

A. Exposition (Statement of themes)
B. Development Section (Development of themes)
A. Recapitulation (Repetition of the exposition themes).

Suite—A composition made up of a number of pieces for solo instrument or orchestra. In a Bach suite the movements are written in different dance forms—allemande, courante, sarabande, gavotte, minuet, gigue.

Symphonic Poem—Composition for orchestra which tells a story through music alone. It is not written in a fixed form like a symphony.

Symphony—Composition for a full orchestra usually in four movements.

I. A movement in Sonata Form usually an "allegro."
II. A movement usually in a slow tempo like an "adagio."
III. minuet or scherzo.
IV. A movement, usually fast, like a rondo.

Tempo—The speed at which music is played.

Theme—The musical idea or melody that forms the basis for variation, development, etc. in a composition.

Trio—A composition for three singers or instruments. The usual combination of instruments is violin, 'cello, and piano.

A trio can also be the middle part of a minuet, scherzo, or march.

Variation—Changing a theme by "dressing it up in different costumes." Sometimes a composition in which there are many variations of a theme is called *variations*. The theme is almost always easy to recognize.

Voice—The instrument of human speech or song. Also a part in a musical piece to be played or sung by one kind of instrument or one level of human voice, in conjunction with other such parts.

Waltz—A dance written in 3/4 time with the accent on the first beat of the measure.

The tempo of the waltz may vary from slow to moderately fast. Schubert, Brahms, and Chopin wrote many waltzes for the piano.

Index